I0448737

JAN. 10

Test Results for Digital Data Acquisition Tool:
Logicube Forensic Talon (Software
Version 2.43)

NCJ 228981

Kristina Rose
Acting Director, National Institute of Justice

This report was prepared for the National Institute of Justice, U.S. Department of Justice, by the Office of Law Enforcement Standards of the National Institute of Standards and Technology under Interagency Agreement 2003–IJ–R–029.

The National Institute of Justice is a component of the Office of Justice Programs, which also includes the Bureau of Justice Assistance, the Bureau of Justice Statistics, the Office of Juvenile Justice and Delinquency Prevention, and the Office for Victims of Crime.

August 2009

Test Results for Digital Data Acquisition Tool:
Logicube Forensic Talon (Software Version 2.43)

**National Institute of
Standards and Technology**
U.S. Department of Commerce

Contents

Introduction

The Computer Forensics Tool Testing (CFTT) program is a joint project of the National Institute of Justice (NIJ), the research and development organization of the U.S. Department of Justice (DOJ), and the National Institute of Standards and Technology's (NIST's) Office of Law Enforcement Standards and Information Technology Laboratory. CFTT is supported by other organizations, including the Federal Bureau of Investigation, the U.S. Department of Defense Cyber Crime Center, U.S. Internal Revenue Service Criminal Investigation Division Electronic Crimes Program, and the U.S. Department of Homeland Security's Bureau of Immigration and Customs Enforcement and U.S. Secret Service. The objective of the CFTT program is to provide measurable assurance to practitioners, researchers, and other applicable users that the tools used in computer forensics investigations provide accurate results. Accomplishing this requires the development of specifications and test methods for computer forensics tools and subsequent testing of specific tools against those specifications.

Test results provide the information necessary for developers to improve tools, users to make informed choices, and the legal community and others to understand the tools' capabilities. The CFTT approach to testing computer forensic tools is based on well-recognized methodologies for conformance and quality testing. The specifications and test methods are posted on the CFTT Web site (http://www.cftt.nist.gov/) for review and comment by the computer forensics community.

This document reports the results from testing the Logicube Forensic Talon, software version 2.43, against the *Digital Data Acquisition Tool Assertions and Test Plan Version 1.0*, available at the CFTT Web site (http://www.cftt.nist.gov/DA-ATP-pc-01.pdf).

Test results from other tools and the CFTT tool methodology can be found on NIJ's computer forensics tool testing Web page, http://www.ojp.usdoj.gov/nij/topics/technology/electronic-crime/cftt.htm.

Test Results for Digital Data Acquisition Tool

Tool Tested: Logicube Talon
Software Version: 2.43

Supplier: Logicube

Address: 19755 Nordhoff Place
                 Chatsworth, CA 91311
Tel: 888–494–8832
Fax: 818–700–8466
WWW: http://www.logicube.com/

1 Results Summary

Except for one test case, DA–01–PCMCIA, the tested tool acquired all visible and hidden sectors completely and accurately from the test media without anomaly. The following anomaly was observed:

- Data was inaccurately acquired over the PCMCIA interface (DA–01–PCMCIA).

2 Test Case Selection

Test cases used to test disk imaging tools are defined in *Digital Data Acquisition Tool Assertions and Test Plan Version 1.0*. To test a tool, test cases are selected from the *Test Plan* document based on the features offered by the tool. Not all test cases or test assertions are appropriate for all tools. There is a core set of base cases (DA–06, DA–07 and DA–08) that are executed for every tool tested. Tool features guide the selection of additional test cases. If a given tool implements a given feature then the test cases linked to that feature are run. Table 1 lists the features available in the Forensic Talon and the linked test cases selected for execution. Table 2 lists the features not available in the Forensic Talon and the test cases not executed.

Table 1 Selected Test Cases

Supported Optional Feature	Cases selected for execution
Create a clone during acquisition	01
Create a truncated clone from a physical device	04
Base Cases	06, 07 & 08
Read error during acquisition	09
Insufficient space for image file	12
Fill excess sectors on a clone acquisition	19

Table 2 Omitted Test Cases

Unsupported Optional Feature	Cases omitted (not executed)
Create an unaligned clone from a digital source	02
Create cylinder aligned clones	03, 15, 21 & 23
Convert an image file from one format to another	26
Destination Device Switching	13
Device I/O error generator available	05, 11 & 18
Fill excess sectors on a clone device	20, 21, 22 & 23
Create a clone from an image file	14 & 17
Create a clone from a subset of an image file	16
Detect a corrupted (or changed) image file	24 & 25

Some test cases have variant forms to accommodate parameters within test assertions. These variations cover the acquisition interface to the source drive and how the tool treats faulty sectors encountered on source media. Acquisition speed was also varied between test cases.

The following source interfaces were tested: ATA28, ATA48, SATA28, SATA48, USB, XUSB, and PCMCIA. These are noted as variations on test cases DA–01, DA–06, and DA–08. See section 4 for a discussion of testing the USB, XUSB, and PCMCIA source interfaces.

For test case DA–09 the Forensic Talon's methods for treating faulty sectors encountered on source media are varied so that reads of faulty sectors are either retried (RETRY) or not retried (SKIP).

The compact flash digital source type was tested in test case DA–07–CF.

Acquisition speeds were varied between UDMA–0, UDMA–3, UDMA–5, and PIO–AUTO.

3 Results by Test Assertion

A test assertion is a verifiable statement about a single condition after an action is performed by the tool under test. A test case usually checks a group of assertions after the action of a single execution of the tool under test. Test assertions are defined and linked to test cases in *Digital Data Acquisition Tool Assertions and Test Plan Version 1.0*. Table 3 summarizes the test results for all the test cases by assertion. The column labeled **Assertions Tested** gives the text of each assertion. The column labeled **Tests** gives the number of test cases that use the given assertion. The column labeled **Anomaly** gives the section number in this report where any observed anomalies are discussed.

See section 2 for a discussion of source access interface and digital source.

Table 3 Assertions Tested

Assertions Tested	Tests	Anomaly
AM-01 The tool uses access interface SRC-AI to access the digital source.	23	
AM-02 The tool acquires digital source DS.	23	
AM-03 The tool executes in execution environment XE.	23	
AM-04 If clone creation is specified, the tool creates a clone of the digital source.	9	
AM-05 If image file creation is specified, the tool creates an image file on file system type FS.	14	
AM-06 All visible sectors are acquired from the digital source.	22	
AM-07 All hidden sectors are acquired from the digital source.	3	
AM-08 All sectors acquired from the digital source are acquired accurately.	22	3.1
AM-09 If unresolved errors occur while reading from the selected digital source, the tool notifies the user of the error type and location within the digital source.	4	
AM-10 If unresolved errors occur while reading from the selected digital source, the tool uses a benign fill in the destination object in place of the inaccessible data.	4	
AO-01 If the tool creates an image file, the data represented by the image file is the same as the data acquired by the tool.	13	
AO-04 If the tool is creating an image file and there is insufficient space on the image destination device to contain the image file, the tool shall notify the user.	1	
AO-05 If the tool creates a multifile image of a requested size then all the individual files shall be no larger than the requested size.	13	
AO-11 If requested, a clone is created during an acquisition of a digital source.	9	
AO-13 A clone is created using access interface DST-AI to write to the clone device.	9	
AO-14 If an unaligned clone is created, each sector written to the clone is accurately written to the same disk address on the clone that the sector occupied on the digital source.	9	
AO-17 If requested, any excess sectors on a clone destination device are not modified.	6	
AO-18 If requested, a benign fill is written to excess sectors of a clone.	1	
AO-19 If there is insufficient space to create a complete clone, a truncated clone is created using all available sectors of the clone device.	1	
AO-20 If a truncated clone is created, the tool notifies the user.	1	
AO-22 If requested, the tool calculates block hashes for a specified block size during an acquisition for each block acquired from the digital source.	5	
AO-23 If the tool logs any log significant	23	

Assertions Tested	Tests	Anomaly
information, the information is accurately recorded in the log file.		
AO-24 If the tool executes in a forensically safe execution environment, the digital source is unchanged by the acquisition process.	23	

Two test assertions only apply in special circumstances. The assertion AO–22 is checked only for tools that create block hashes. For the Forensic Talon block hash computation was only tested in five test cases. The assertion AO–24 is only checked if the tool is executed in a run time environment that does not modify attached storage devices, such as MS DOS. In normal operation an imaging tool is used in conjunction with a write block device to protect the source drive; however a blocker was not used during the tests so that assertion AO–24 could be checked. Table 4 lists the assertions that were not tested, usually due to the tool not supporting some optional feature, e.g., creation of cylinder aligned clones.

Table 4 Assertions not Tested

Assertions not Tested
AO-02 If an image file format is specified, the tool creates an image file in the specified format.
AO-03 If there is an error while writing the image file, the tool notifies the user.
AO-06 If the tool performs an image file integrity check on an image file that has not been changed since the file was created, the tool shall notify the user that the image file has not been changed.
AO-07 If the tool performs an image file integrity check on an image file that has been changed since the file was created, the tool shall notify the user that the image file has been changed.
AO-08 If the tool performs an image file integrity check on an image file that has been changed since the file was created, the tool shall notify the user of the affected locations.
AO-09 If the tool converts a source image file from one format to a target image file in another format, the acquired data represented in the target image file is the same as the acquired data in the source image file.
AO-10 If there is insufficient space to contain all files of a multifile image and if destination device switching is supported, the image is continued on another device.
AO-12 If requested, a clone is created from an image file.
AO-15 If an aligned clone is created, each sector within a contiguous span of sectors from the source is accurately written to the same disk address on the clone device relative to the start of the span as the sector occupied on the original digital source. A span of sectors is defined to be either a mountable partition or a contiguous sequence of sectors not part of a mountable partition. Extended partitions, which may contain both mountable partitions and unallocated sectors, are not mountable partitions.
AO-16 If a subset of an image or acquisition is specified, all the subset is cloned.
AO-21 If there is a write error during clone creation, the tool notifies the user.

3.1 PCMCIA Acquisition

In test case DA–01–PCMCIA where the PCMCIA interface was used to acquire a laptop's internal hard drive the tool did not acquire all sectors accurately. 220,416 sectors were not acquired. In their place, sectors from earlier and later parts of the source drive were written to the destination drive. The acquisition hash computed by the tool did not match the source drive's reference hash.

4 Testing Environment

The tests were run in the NIST CFTT lab. This section describes the test computers available for testing, using the support software, and notes on other test hardware.

The majority of the tests were run using a standard configuration of the Forensic Talon and the natively supported ATA and SATA interfaces. Three test cases tested alternate configurations and interfaces. Test case DA–01–USB tested the acquisition of USB devices using the Logicube Omni Port adapter. DA–01–PCMCIA and DA–01–XUSB acquired devices over the PCMCIA and USB interfaces using vendor-supplied boot CDs and DOS programs.

4.1 Test Computers

For most test cases the Forensic Talon images a drive without assistance from a computer, however for test cases DA–01–PCMCIA and DA–01–XUSB the test computer, Chip, was used.

Chip has the following configuration:

Dell Latitude D800
Phoenix Technologies BIOS Revision A09
Intel® Pentium™ M CPU 1.7Ghz
Intel® 855PM chipset
2GB RAM
Samsung SN–324S CDRW/DVD-ROM drive
1 PCMCIA port
3 USB 2.0 ports
1 IEEE 1394 port

4.2 Support Software

A package of programs to support test analysis, FS-TST Release 2.0, was used. The software can be obtained from: http://www.cftt.nist.gov/diskimaging/fs-tst20.zip.

4.3 Test Drive Creation

There are three ways that a hard drive may be used in a tool test case: as a source drive that is imaged by the tool, as a media drive that contains image files created by the tool under test, or as a destination drive on which the tool under test creates a clone of the source drive. In addition to the operating system drive formatting tools, some tools (diskwipe and diskhash) from the FS-TST package are used to setup test drives.

To setup a media drive, the drive is formatted with one of the supported file systems. A media drive may be used in several test cases.

The setup of most source drives follows the same general procedure, but there are several steps that may be varied depending on the needs of the test case.
1. The drive is filled with known data by the **diskwipe** program from FS-TST. The **diskwipe** program writes the sector address to each sector in both C/H/S and LBA format. The remainder of the sector bytes is set to a constant fill value unique for each drive. The fill value is noted in the **diskwipe** tool log file.
2. The drive may be formatted with partitions as required for the test case.
3. An operating system may optionally be installed.
4. A set of reference hashes is created by the FS-TST **diskhash** tool. These include both SHA1 and MD5 hashes. In addition to full drive hashes, hashes of each partition may also be computed.
5. If the drive is intended for hidden area tests (DA–08), an HPA, a DCO or both may be created. The **diskhash** tool is then used to calculate reference hashes of just the visible sectors of the drive.

The source drives for DA–09 are created such that there is a consistent set of faulty sectors on the drive. Each of these source drives is initialized with **diskwipe** and then their faulty sectors are activated. For each of these source drives, a second drive of the same size with the same content as the faulty sector drive, but with no faulty sectors serves as a reference drive for images made from the faulty drive.

To setup a destination drive, the drive is filled with known data by the **diskwipe** program from FS-TST. Partitions may be created if the test case involves restoring from the image of a logical acquire.

4.4 Test Drive Analysis

For test cases (DA–01, DA–09, and DA–19) that create on a destination drive a cloned version of a source drive, the source is compared using the FS-TST programs **diskcmp** (for an entire drive) and **partcmp** (for a single partition) to the destination and any differences are noted. For test case DA–09, using a drive with known bad sectors, the program **anabad** is used to compare the bad sector reference drive to a cloned version of the of the bad sector drive.

For test cases such as DA–06 and DA–07 the acquisition hash is compared to the reference hash of the source to check that the source is completely and accurately acquired.

4.5 Note on Test Drives

The testing uses several test drives from a variety of vendors. The drives are identified by an external label that consists of a two digit hexadecimal value and an optional tag, e.g., 25–SATA. The combination of hex value and tag serves as a unique identifier for each drive. The two digit hex value is used by the FS-TST **diskwipe** program as a sector fill value. The FS-TST compare tools, **diskcmp** and **partcmp,** count sectors that are filled with the source and destination fill values on a destination that is larger than the original source.

5   Test Results

The main item of interest for interpreting the test results is determining the conformance of the device with the test assertions. Conformance with each assertion tested by a given test case is evaluated by examining the **Log File Highlights** box of the test report summary.

5.1 Test Results Report Key

A summary of the actual test results is presented in this report. The following table presents a description of each section of the test report summary. The Tester Name, Test Host, Test Date, Drives, Source Setup and Log Highlights sections for each test case are populated by excerpts taken from the logfiles produced by the tool under test and the FS-TST tools that were executed in support of test case setup and analysis.

Heading	Description
First Line:	Test case ID, name, and version of tool tested.
Case Summary:	Test case summary from *Digital Data Acquisition Tool Assertions and Test Plan Version 1.0.*
Assertions:	The test assertions applicable to the test case, selected from *Digital Data Acquisition Tool Assertions and Test Plan Version 1.0.*
Tester Name:	Name or initials of person executing test procedure.
Test Host:	Host computer executing the test.
Test Date:	Time and date that test was started.
Drives:	Source drive (the drive acquired), destination drive (if a clone is created) and media drive (to contain a created image).
Source Setup:	Layout of partitions on the source drive and the expected hash of the drive.
Log Highlights:	Information extracted from various log files to illustrate conformance or nonconformance to the test assertions.
Results	Expected and actual results for each assertion tested.
Analysis	Whether or not the expected results were achieved.

5.2 Test Details

5.2.1 DA-01-ATA28

Test Case DA-01-ATA28 F-TALON V2.43	
Case Summary:	DA-01 Acquire a physical device using access interface AI to an unaligned clone.
Assertions:	AM-01 The tool uses access interface SRC-AI to access the digital source. AM-02 The tool acquires digital source DS. AM-03 The tool executes in execution environment XE. AM-04 If clone creation is specified, the tool creates a clone of the digital source. AM-06 All visible sectors are acquired from the digital source. AM-08 All sectors acquired from the digital source are acquired accurately. AO-11 If requested, a clone is created during an acquisition of a digital source. AO-13 A clone is created using access interface DST-AI to write to the clone device. AO-14 If an unaligned clone is created, each sector written to the clone is accurately written to the same disk address on the clone that the sector occupied on the digital source. AO-17 If requested, any excess sectors on a clone destination device are not modified. AO-22 If requested, the tool calculates block hashes for a specified block size during an acquisition for each block acquired from the digital source. AO-23 If the tool logs any log significant information, the information is accurately recorded in the log file. AO-24 If the tool executes in a forensically safe execution environment, the digital source is unchanged by the acquisition process.
Tester Name:	brl
Test Host:	Athos
Test Date:	Wed Oct 17 10:06:36 2007
Drives:	src(43) dst (23-SATA) other (none)

Source Setup:	src hash (SHA256): < 2658F47603DE6B1D883B64823E9733F578658D08D06A4BB8C053C4F57BDC615E >
	src hash (SHA1): < 888E2E7F7AD237DC7A732281DD93F325065E5871 >
	src hash (MD5): < BC39C3F7EE7A50E77B9BA1E65A5AEEF7 >
	78125000 total sectors (40000000000 bytes)
	Model (0BB-75JHC0) serial # (WD-WMAMC46588)
	<pre>N Start LBA Length Start C/H/S End C/H/S boot Partition type
	 1 P 000000063 020980827 0000/001/01 1023/254/63 0C Fat32X
	 2 X 020980890 057143205 1023/000/01 1023/254/63 0F extended
	 3 S 000000063 000032067 1023/001/01 1023/254/63 01 Fat12
	 4 x 000032130 002104515 1023/000/01 1023/254/63 05 extended
	 5 S 000000063 002104452 1023/001/01 1023/254/63 06 Fat16
	 6 x 002136645 004192965 1023/000/01 1023/254/63 05 extended
	 7 S 000000063 004192902 1023/001/01 1023/254/63 16 other
	 8 x 006329610 008401995 1023/000/01 1023/254/63 05 extended
	 9 S 000000063 008401932 1023/001/01 1023/254/63 0B Fat32
	10 x 014731605 010490445 1023/000/01 1023/254/63 05 extended
	11 S 000000063 010490382 1023/001/01 1023/254/63 83 Linux
	12 x 025222050 004209030 1023/000/01 1023/254/63 05 extended
	13 S 000000063 004208967 1023/001/01 1023/254/63 82 Linux swap
	14 x 029431080 027712125 1023/000/01 1023/254/63 05 extended
	15 S 000000063 027712062 1023/001/01 1023/254/63 07 NTFS
	16 S 000000000 000000000 0000/000/00 0000/000/00 00 empty entry
	17 P 000000000 000000000 0000/000/00 0000/000/00 00 empty entry
	18 P 000000000 000000000 0000/000/00 0000/000/00 00 empty entry
	 1 020980827 sectors 10742183424 bytes
	 3 000032067 sectors 16418304 bytes
	 5 002104452 sectors 1077479424 bytes
	 7 004192902 sectors 2146765824 bytes
	 9 008401932 sectors 4301789184 bytes
	11 010490382 sectors 5371075584 bytes
	13 004208967 sectors 2154991104 bytes
	15 027712062 sectors 14188575744 bytes</pre>

Log Highlights:	Destination setup
	156301488 sectors wiped with 23
	
	Comparision of original to clone Drive
	Sectors compared: 78125000
	Sectors match: 78125000
	Sectors differ: 0
	Bytes differ: 0
	Diffs range
	Source (78125000) has 78176488 fewer sectors than destination (156301488)
	Zero fill: 0
	Src Byte fill (43): 0
	Dst Byte fill (23): 78176488
	Other fill: 0
	Other no fill: 0
	Zero fill range:
	Src fill range:
	Dst fill range: 78125000-156301487
	Other fill range:
	Other not filled range:
	0 source read errors, 0 destination read errors
	
	***** FORENSIC TALON Serial No.: 15881 Software: V2.43 *****
	                SESSION SETTINGS
	     Operating Mode: Capture Address Mode: LBA
	     Verify : SHA-256 Speed : UDMA-0
	     Connection : Direct
	            100% MIRROR COPY OF THE SUSPECT DRIVE HAS BEEN
	            SUCCESSFULLY EXECUTED ON THE EVIDENCE DRIVE!
	      Operator declined FULL and remainder Destination Drive erase!
	************************* SOURCE DRIVE *************************
	                Physical Characteristics
	    Drive Model: WDC WD400BB-75JHC0
	       Serial: WD-WMAMC4658888
	     Cylinders Heads Sectors Total Sectors Drive Size
	      77504 16 63 78125000 37.3 GB
	        Computed SHA-256 Value:
	     2658F47603DE6B1D883B64823E9733F578658D08D06A4BB8C053C4F57BDC615E
	             Skipped Sectors: 0
	********************** DESTINATION DRIVE **********************
	                Physical Characteristics
	    Drive Model: ST380013AS
	       Serial: 5JVCYJCF
	     Cylinders Heads Sectors Total Sectors Drive Size
	      155061 16 63 156301488 74.5 GB
	        Computed SHA-256 Value: NONE
	                Skipped Sectors: 0
	Settings: error skip
	speed UDMA-0

Results:	

Assertion & Expected Result	Actual Result
AM-01 Source acquired using interface AI.	as expected
AM-02 Source is type DS.	as expected
AM-03 Execution environment is XE.	as expected
AM-04 A clone is created.	as expected
AM-06 All visible sectors acquired.	as expected
AM-08 All sectors accurately acquired.	as expected
AO-11 A clone is created during acquisition.	as expected
AO-13 Clone created using interface AI.	as expected
AO-14 An unaligned clone is created.	as expected
AO-17 Excess sectors are unchanged.	as expected
AO-22 Tool calculates hashes by block.	option not tested
AO-23 Logged information is correct.	as expected
AO-24 Source is unchanged by acquisition.	as expected

Analysis:	Expected results achieved

5.2.2 DA-01-ATA48

Test Case DA-01-ATA48 F-TALON V2.43	
Case Summary:	DA-01 Acquire a physical device using access interface AI to an unaligned clone.
Assertions:	AM-01 The tool uses access interface SRC-AI to access the digital source. AM-02 The tool acquires digital source DS. AM-03 The tool executes in execution environment XE. AM-04 If clone creation is specified, the tool creates a clone of the digital source. AM-06 All visible sectors are acquired from the digital source. AM-08 All sectors acquired from the digital source are acquired accurately. AO-11 If requested, a clone is created during an acquisition of a digital source. AO-13 A clone is created using access interface DST-AI to write to the clone device. AO-14 If an unaligned clone is created, each sector written to the clone is accurately written to the same disk address on the clone that the sector occupied on the digital source. AO-17 If requested, any excess sectors on a clone destination device are not modified. AO-22 If requested, the tool calculates block hashes for a specified block size during an acquisition for each block acquired from the digital source. AO-23 If the tool logs any log significant information, the information is accurately recorded in the log file. AO-24 If the tool executes in a forensically safe execution environment, the digital source is unchanged by the acquisition process.
Tester Name:	brl
Test Host:	Athos
Test Date:	Wed Oct 17 16:48:21 2007
Drives:	src(4C) dst (2B-IDE) other (none)
Source Setup:	src hash (SHA1): < 8FF620D2BEDCCAFE8412EDAAD56C8554F872EFBF > src hash (MD5): < D10F763B56D4CEBA2D1311C61F9FB382 > 390721968 total sectors (200049647616 bytes) 24320/254/63 (max cyl/hd values) 24321/255/63 (number of cyl/hd) IDE disk: Model (WDC WD2000JB-00KFA0) serial # (WD-WMAMR1031111) N Start LBA Length Start C/H/S End C/H/S boot Partition type 1 P 000000063 390700737 0000/001/01 1023/254/63 Boot 07 NTFS 2 P 000000000 000000000 0000/000/00 0000/000/00 00 empty entry 3 P 000000000 000000000 0000/000/00 0000/000/00 00 empty entry 4 P 000000000 000000000 0000/000/00 0000/000/00 00 empty entry 1 390700737 sectors 200038777344 bytes
Log Highlights:	Destination setup 490234752 sectors wiped with 2B Comparision of original to clone Drive Sectors compared: 390721968 Sectors match: 390721968 Sectors differ: 0 Bytes differ: 0 Diffs range Source (390721968) has 99512784 fewer sectors than destination (490234752) Zero fill: 0 Src Byte fill (4C): 0 Dst Byte fill (2B): 99512784 Other fill: 0 Other no fill: 0 Zero fill range: Src fill range: Dst fill range: 390721968-490234751 Other fill range: Other not filled range: 0 source read errors, 0 destination read errors ***** FORENSIC TALON Serial No.: 15881 Software: V2.43 ***** SESSION SETTINGS

Test Case DA-01-ATA48 F-TALON V2.43

```
            Operating Mode: Capture          Address Mode: LBA
            Verify        : HW-MD5          Speed  : UDMA-4
            Connection    : Direct
                    100% MIRROR COPY OF THE SUSPECT DRIVE HAS BEEN
                      SUCCESSFULLY EXECUTED ON THE EVIDENCE DRIVE!
            Operator declined FULL and remainder Destination Drive erase!
            *************************  SOURCE DRIVE  *************************
                            Physical Characteristics
            Drive Model: WDC WD2000JB-00KFA0
                Serial: WD-WMAMR1031111
                Cylinders    Heads    Sectors    Total Sectors    Drive Size
                  387621      16        63         390721968        186.3 GB
                    Computed MD5 Value: D10F763B 56D4CEBA 2D1311C6 1F9FB382
                            Skipped Sectors: 0
            ************************  DESTINATION DRIVE  ************************
                            Physical Characteristics
            Drive Model: Maxtor 7Y250P0
                Serial: Y63DQXCE
                Cylinders    Heads    Sectors    Total Sectors    Drive Size
                  486344      16        63         490234752        233.8 GB
                    Computed SHA-256 Value:  NONE
                            Skipped Sectors: 0
        Settings: error skip
        speed UDMA-5
```

Results:	

Assertion & Expected Result	Actual Result
AM-01 Source acquired using interface AI.	as expected
AM-02 Source is type DS.	as expected
AM-03 Execution environment is XE.	as expected
AM-04 A clone is created.	as expected
AM-06 All visible sectors acquired.	as expected
AM-08 All sectors accurately acquired.	as expected
AO-11 A clone is created during acquisition.	as expected
AO-13 Clone created using interface AI.	as expected
AO-14 An unaligned clone is created.	as expected
AO-17 Excess sectors are unchanged.	as expected
AO-22 Tool calculates hashes by block.	option not tested
AO-23 Logged information is correct.	as expected
AO-24 Source is unchanged by acquisition.	as expected

Analysis:	Expected results achieved

5.2.3 DA-01-PCMCIA

Test Case DA-01-□C□C□A F-TALON V2.43	
Case Summary:	DA-01 Acquire a physical device using access interface AI to an unaligned clone.
Assertions:	AM-01 The tool uses access interface SRC-AI to access the digital source.
	AM-02 The tool acquires digital source DS.
	AM-03 The tool executes in execution environment XE.
	AM-04 If clone creation is specified, the tool creates a clone of the digital source.
	AM-06 All visible sectors are acquired from the digital source.
	AM-08 All sectors acquired from the digital source are acquired accurately.
	AO-11 If requested, a clone is created during an acquisition of a digital source.
	AO-13 A clone is created using access interface DST-AI to write to the clone device.
	AO-14 If an unaligned clone is created, each sector written to the clone is accurately written to the same disk address on the clone that the sector occupied on the digital source.
	AO-17 If requested, any excess sectors on a clone destination device are not modified.
	AO-22 If requested, the tool calculates block hashes for a specified block size during an acquisition for each block acquired from the digital source.
	AO-23 If the tool logs any log significant information, the information is accurately recorded in the log file.
	AO-24 If the tool executes in a forensically safe execution environment, the digital source is unchanged by the acquisition process.
Tester Name:	brl
Test Host:	Athos
Test Date:	Wed Nov 14 09:58:03 2007
Drives:	src(09-LAP) dst (8C) other (none)
Source Setup:	src hash (SHA1): < 118459903C8BB9E6D668DBFDD5D54832BE88E029 >
	src hash (MD5): < 602C740729A16808E42696C1D9C93C96 >
	195371568 total sectors (100030242816 bytes)
	12160/254/63 (max cyl/hd values)
	12161/255/63 (number of cyl/hd)
	Model (A) serial # (5MH0KZ)
	This drive has a DCO of 8000001 sectors
	The hashes with DCO in place are:
	MD5: 00A81DE5822E84E9606DEF68D9D17367
	SHA1: 7A247D230345EFC1A412586A83AA6AD66266D2B1
Log Highlights:	Destination setup
	39102336 sectors wiped with 8C
	Comparision of original to clone Drive
	Sectors compared: 8000001
	Sectors match: 7779585
	Sectors differ: 220416
	Bytes differ: 2200591
	Diffs range 8704-8959, 17920-18175, 27136-27391, 36352-36607, 45824-46079, 55040-55295, 64256-64511, 73728-73983, 82944-83199, 92160-92415, 101376-101631, 110848-111103, 120064-120319, 129280-129535, 138496-138751, 147968-148223, 157184-157439, 166400-166655, 175872-176127, 185088-185343. . . + 215296 more
	Source (8000001) has 31102335 fewer sectors than destination (39102336)
	Zero fill: 0
	Src Byte fill (09): 0
	Dst Byte fill (8C): 31102335
	Other fill: 0
	Other no fill: 0
	Zero fill range:
	Src fill range:
	Dst fill range: 8000001-39102335
	Other fill range:

```
                  Other not filled range:
                  0 source read errors, 0 destination read errors

                  *****     FORENSIC TALON     Serial No.: 15881  Software: V2.43    *****
                                      SESSION SETTINGS
                    Operating Mode: Capture          Address Mode: LBA
                    Verify      : HW-MD5             Speed   : PIO-MEDIUM
                    Connection  : Direct
                          100% MIRROR COPY OF THE SUSPECT DRIVE HAS BEEN
                           SUCCESSFULLY EXECUTED ON THE EVIDENCE DRIVE!
                      Operator declined FULL and remainder Destination Drive erase!
                  *************************   SOURCE DRIVE   *************************
                              Physical Characteristics
                  Drive Model: ST910021A
                      Serial: 5MH0KZYH
                    Cylinders   Heads   Sectors    Total Sectors    Drive Size
                      7936        16      63         8000001          3.8 GB
                        Computed MD5 Value: 552B58CF 8C7378F8 D5738E1D FE9ACDBC
                              Skipped Sectors: 0
                  **********************  DESTINATION DRIVE  **********************
                              Physical Characteristics
                  Drive Model: WDC WD200EB-00CSF0
                      Serial: WD-WMAAV2431177
                    Cylinders   Heads   Sectors    Total Sectors    Drive Size
                      38792       16      63         39102336         18.6 GB
                        Computed SHA-256 Value:  NONE
                              Skipped Sectors: 0
                  Settings: error skip
                  speed PIO-MEDIUM
```

Results:	

Assertion & Expected Result	Actual Result
AM-01 Source acquired using interface AI.	as expected
AM-02 Source is type DS.	as expected
AM-03 Execution environment is XE.	as expected
AM-04 A clone is created.	as expected
AM-06 All visible sectors acquired.	some sectors omitted
AM-08 All sectors accurately acquired.	some sectors differ
AO-11 A clone is created during acquisition.	as expected
AO-13 Clone created using interface AI.	as expected
AO-14 An unaligned clone is created.	as expected
AO-17 Excess sectors are unchanged.	as expected
AO-22 Tool calculates hashes by block.	option not tested
AO-23 Logged information is correct.	as expected
AO-24 Source is unchanged by acquisition.	not checked

Analysis:	Expected results not achieved

5.2.4 DA-01-SATA28

Test Case DA-01-□ATA28 F-TALON V2.43	
Case Summary:	DA-01 Acquire a physical device using access interface AI to an unaligned clone.
Assertions:	AM-01 The tool uses access interface SRC-AI to access the digital source. AM-02 The tool acquires digital source DS. AM-03 The tool executes in execution environment XE. AM-04 If clone creation is specified, the tool creates a clone of the digital source. AM-06 All visible sectors are acquired from the digital source. AM-08 All sectors acquired from the digital source are acquired accurately. AO-11 If requested, a clone is created during an acquisition of a digital source. AO-13 A clone is created using access interface DST-AI to write to the clone device. AO-14 If an unaligned clone is created, each sector written to the clone is accurately written to the same disk address on the clone that the sector occupied on the digital source. AO-17 If requested, any excess sectors on a clone destination device are not modified. AO-22 If requested, the tool calculates block hashes for a specified block size during an acquisition for each block acquired from the digital source. AO-23 If the tool logs any log significant information, the information is accurately recorded in the log file. AO-24 If the tool executes in a forensically safe execution environment, the digital source is unchanged by the acquisition process.
Tester Name:	brl
Test Host:	Athos
Test Date:	Thu Oct 18 13:07:27 2007
Drives:	src(07-SATA) dst (23-IDE) other (none)
Source Setup:	src hash (SHA1): < 655E9BDDB36A3F9C5C4CC8BF32B8C5B41AF9F52E > src hash (MD5): < 2EAF712DAD80F66E30DEA00365B4579B > 156301488 total sectors (80026361856 bytes) Model (WDC WD800JD-32HK) serial # (WD-WMAJ91510044) N Start LBA Length Start C/H/S End C/H/S boot Partition type 1 P 000000063 156280257 0000/001/01 1023/254/63 Boot 07 NTFS 2 P 000000000 000000000 0000/000/00 0000/000/00 00 empty entry 3 P 000000000 000000000 0000/000/00 0000/000/00 00 empty entry 4 P 000000000 000000000 0000/000/00 0000/000/00 00 empty entry 1 156280257 sectors 80015491584 bytes

Log Highlights:	Destination setup
	195813072 sectors wiped with 23
	
	Comparision of original to clone Drive
	Sectors compared: 156301488
	Sectors match: 156301488
	Sectors differ: 0
	Bytes differ: 0
	Diffs range
	Source (156301488) has 39511584 fewer sectors than destination (195813072)
	Zero fill: 0
	Src Byte fill (07): 0
	Dst Byte fill (23): 39511584
	Other fill: 0
	Other no fill: 0
	Zero fill range:
	Src fill range:
	Dst fill range: 156301488-195813071
	Other fill range:
	Other not filled range:
	0 source read errors, 0 destination read errors
	
	***** FORENSIC TALON Serial No.: 15881 Software: V2.43 *****
	                         SESSION SETTINGS
	    Operating Mode: Capture Address Mode: LBA
	    Verify : MD5+V Speed : UDMA-1

```
Test Case DA-01- ATA28 F-TALON V2.43
                    Connection  : Direct
                       100% MIRROR COPY OF THE SUSPECT DRIVE HAS BEEN
                         SUCCESSFULLY EXECUTED ON THE EVIDENCE DRIVE!
                    Operator declined FULL and remainder Destination Drive erase!
                *************************  SOURCE DRIVE  *************************
                               Physical Characteristics
                   Drive Model: WDC WD800JD-32HKA0
                      Serial: WD-WMAJ91510044
                   Cylinders    Heads    Sectors     Total Sectors    Drive Size
                     155061      16        63          156301488        74.5 GB
                       Computed MD5 Value: 2EAF712D AD80F66E 30DEA003 65B4579B
                               Skipped Sectors: 0
                ***********************  DESTINATION DRIVE  **********************
                               Physical Characteristics
                   Drive Model: Maxtor 6L100P0
                      Serial: L26YGVQG
                   Cylinders    Heads    Sectors     Total Sectors    Drive Size
                     194259      16        63          195813072        93.4 GB
                       Computed MD5 Value: 2EAF712D AD80F66E 30DEA003 65B4579B
                               Skipped Sectors: 0
            Settings: error skip
            speed UDMA-3
```

Results:		
	Assertion & Expected Result	Actual Result
	AM-01 Source acquired using interface AI.	as expected
	AM-02 Source is type DS.	as expected
	AM-03 Execution environment is XE.	as expected
	AM-04 A clone is created.	as expected
	AM-06 All visible sectors acquired.	as expected
	AM-08 All sectors accurately acquired.	as expected
	AO-11 A clone is created during acquisition.	as expected
	AO-13 Clone created using interface AI.	as expected
	AO-14 An unaligned clone is created.	as expected
	AO-17 Excess sectors are unchanged.	as expected
	AO-22 Tool calculates hashes by block.	option not tested
	AO-23 Logged information is correct.	as expected
	AO-24 Source is unchanged by acquisition.	as expected

Analysis:	Expected results achieved

5.2.5 DA-01-SATA48

Test Case DA-01-☐ATA48 F-TALON V2.43	
Case Summary:	DA-01 Acquire a physical device using access interface AI to an unaligned clone.
Assertions:	AM-01 The tool uses access interface SRC-AI to access the digital source. AM-02 The tool acquires digital source DS. AM-03 The tool executes in execution environment XE. AM-04 If clone creation is specified, the tool creates a clone of the digital source. AM-06 All visible sectors are acquired from the digital source. AM-08 All sectors acquired from the digital source are acquired accurately. AO-11 If requested, a clone is created during an acquisition of a digital source. AO-13 A clone is created using access interface DST-AI to write to the clone device. AO-14 If an unaligned clone is created, each sector written to the clone is accurately written to the same disk address on the clone that the sector occupied on the digital source. AO-17 If requested, any excess sectors on a clone destination device are not modified. AO-22 If requested, the tool calculates block hashes for a specified block size during an acquisition for each block acquired from the digital source. AO-23 If the tool logs any log significant information, the information is accurately recorded in the log file. AO-24 If the tool executes in a forensically safe execution environment, the digital source is unchanged by the acquisition process.
Tester Name:	brl
Test Host:	Athos
Test Date:	Fri Oct 19 11:38:43 2007
Drives:	src(0D-SATA) dst (0B-SATA) other (none)
Source Setup:	src hash (SHA1): < BAAD80E8781E55F2E3EF528CA73BD41D228C1377 > src hash (MD5): < 1FA7C3CBE60EB9E89863DED2411E40C9 > 488397168 total sectors (250059350016 bytes) 30400/254/63 (max cyl/hd values) 30401/255/63 (number of cyl/hd) Model (WDC WD2500JD-22F) serial # (WD-WMAEH2678216) N Start LBA Length Start C/H/S End C/H/S boot Partition type 1 P 000000063 488375937 0000/001/01 1023/254/63 Boot 07 NTFS 2 P 000000000 000000000 0000/000/00 0000/000/00 00 empty entry 3 P 000000000 000000000 0000/000/00 0000/000/00 00 empty entry 4 P 000000000 000000000 0000/000/00 0000/000/00 00 empty entry 1 488375937 sectors 250048479744 bytes

Log Highlights:	Destination setup
	488397168 sectors wiped with B
	
	Comparision of original to clone Drive
	Sectors compared: 488397168
	Sectors match: 488397168
	Sectors differ: 0
	Bytes differ: 0
	Diffs range
	0 source read errors, 0 destination read errors
	
	***** FORENSIC TALON Serial No.: 15881 Software: V2.43 *****
	                  SESSION SETTINGS
	   Operating Mode: Capture Address Mode: LBA
	   Verify : HW-MD5 Speed : UDMA-4
	   Connection : Direct
	           100% MIRROR COPY OF THE SUSPECT DRIVE HAS BEEN
	         SUCCESSFULLY EXECUTED ON THE EVIDENCE DRIVE!
	          No Destination Drive erase required!
	************************* SOURCE DRIVE *************************
	              Physical Characteristics
	   Drive Model: WDC WD2500JD-22FYB0
	     Serial: WD-WMAEH2678216
	   Cylinders Heads Sectors Total Sectors Drive Size

```
Test Case DA-01-□ATA48 F-TALON V2.43
          484521        16       63        488397168        232.9 GB
             Computed MD5 Value: 1FA7C3CB E60EB9E8 9863DED2 411E40C9
                         Skipped Sectors: 0
      ************************  DESTINATION DRIVE  ***********************
                        Physical Characteristics
           Drive Model: WDC WD2500JD-22FYB0
              Serial: WD-WMAEH2677545
           Cylinders    Heads    Sectors     Total Sectors    Drive Size
            484521        16       63        488397168        232.9 GB
             Computed SHA-256 Value:  NONE
                         Skipped Sectors: 0
      Settings: error skip
      speed UDMA-5
```

Assertion & Expected Result	Actual Result
AM-01 Source acquired using interface AI.	as expected
AM-02 Source is type DS.	as expected
AM-03 Execution environment is XE.	as expected
AM-04 A clone is created.	as expected
AM-06 All visible sectors acquired.	as expected
AM-08 All sectors accurately acquired.	as expected
AO-11 A clone is created during acquisition.	as expected
AO-13 Clone created using interface AI.	as expected
AO-14 An unaligned clone is created.	as expected
AO-17 Excess sectors are unchanged.	as expected
AO-22 Tool calculates hashes by block.	option not tested
AO-23 Logged information is correct.	as expected
AO-24 Source is unchanged by acquisition.	as expected

Results: (see table above)

Analysis: Expected results achieved

5.2.6 DA-01-USB

Test Case DA-01-□□□ F-TALON V2.43	
Case Summary:	DA-01 Acquire a physical device using access interface AI to an unaligned clone.
Assertions:	AM-01 The tool uses access interface SRC-AI to access the digital source. AM-02 The tool acquires digital source DS. AM-03 The tool executes in execution environment XE. AM-04 If clone creation is specified, the tool creates a clone of the digital source. AM-06 All visible sectors are acquired from the digital source. AM-08 All sectors acquired from the digital source are acquired accurately. AO-11 If requested, a clone is created during an acquisition of a digital source. AO-13 A clone is created using access interface DST-AI to write to the clone device. AO-14 If an unaligned clone is created, each sector written to the clone is accurately written to the same disk address on the clone that the sector occupied on the digital source. AO-17 If requested, any excess sectors on a clone destination device are not modified. AO-22 If requested, the tool calculates block hashes for a specified block size during an acquisition for each block acquired from the digital source. AO-23 If the tool logs any log significant information, the information is accurately recorded in the log file. AO-24 If the tool executes in a forensically safe execution environment, the digital source is unchanged by the acquisition process.
Tester Name:	brl
Test Host:	Athos
Test Date:	Wed Oct 31 15:30:12 2007
Drives:	src(D5-THUMB) dst (22-SATA) other (none)
Source Setup:	src hash (SHA1): < D68520EF74A336E49DCCF83815B7B08FDC53E38A > src hash (MD5): < C843593624B2B3B878596D8760B19954 > 505856 total sectors (258998272 bytes) Model (usb2.0Flash Disk) serial # () N Start LBA Length Start C/H/S End C/H/S boot Partition type 1 P 778135908 1141509631 0357/116/40 0357/032/45 Boot 72 other 2 P 168689522 1936028240 0288/115/43 0367/114/50 Boot 65 other 3 P 1869881465 1936028192 0366/032/33 0357/032/43 Boot 79 other 4 P 2885681152 000055499 0372/097/50 0000/010/00 Boot 0D other 1 1141509631 sectors 584452931072 bytes 2 1936028240 sectors 991246458880 bytes 3 1936028192 sectors 991246434304 bytes 4 000055499 sectors 28415488 bytes
Log Highlights:	Destination setup 156301488 sectors wiped with 22 Comparision of original to clone Drive Sectors compared: 505856 Sectors match: 505856 Sectors differ: 0 Bytes differ: 0 Diffs range Source (505856) has 155795632 fewer sectors than destination (156301488) Zero fill: 0 Src Byte fill (D5): 0 Dst Byte fill (22): 155795632 Other fill: 0 Other no fill: 0 Zero fill range: Src fill range: Dst fill range: 505856-156301487 Other fill range: Other not filled range: 0 source read errors, 0 destination read errors ***** FORENSIC TALON Serial No.: 15881 Software: V2.43 *****

```
                          SESSION SETTINGS
      Operating Mode: Capture          Address Mode: LBA
      Verify      : HW-MD5              Speed  : PIO-AUTO
      Connection  : Direct
                 100% MIRROR COPY OF THE SUSPECT DRIVE HAS BEEN
                 SUCCESSFULLY EXECUTED ON THE EVIDENCE DRIVE!
          Operator declined FULL and remainder Destination Drive erase!
      *************************    SOURCE DRIVE    *************************
                       Physical Characteristics
      Drive Model: CRUCIAL usb2.0Flash Disk
          Serial:
          Cylinders    Heads    Sectors    Total Sectors    Drive Size
            501         16        63          505856          0.2 GB
            Computed MD5 Value: C8435936 24B2B3B8 78596D87 60B19954
                         Skipped Sectors: 0
      ***********************   DESTINATION DRIVE   ***********************
                       Physical Characteristics
      Drive Model: ST380013AS
          Serial: 5JVCQ731
          Cylinders    Heads    Sectors    Total Sectors    Drive Size
           155061        16        63         156301488        74.5 GB
            Computed SHA-256 Value:  NONE
                         Skipped Sectors: 0
      Settings: error skip
      speed PIO-AUTO
```

	Assertion & Expected Result	Actual Result
Results:	AM-01 Source acquired using interface AI.	as expected
	AM-02 Source is type DS.	as expected
	AM-03 Execution environment is XE.	as expected
	AM-04 A clone is created.	as expected
	AM-06 All visible sectors acquired.	as expected
	AM-08 All sectors accurately acquired.	as expected
	AO-11 A clone is created during acquisition.	as expected
	AO-13 Clone created using interface AI.	as expected
	AO-14 An unaligned clone is created.	as expected
	AO-17 Excess sectors are unchanged.	as expected
	AO-22 Tool calculates hashes by block.	option not tested
	AO-23 Logged information is correct.	as expected
	AO-24 Source is unchanged by acquisition.	as expected
Analysis:	Expected results achieved	

5.2.7 DA-01-XUSB

Test Case DA-01-XUSB F-TALON V2.43	
Case Summary:	DA-01 Acquire a physical device using access interface AI to an unaligned clone.
Assertions:	AM-01 The tool uses access interface SRC-AI to access the digital source. AM-02 The tool acquires digital source DS. AM-03 The tool executes in execution environment XE. AM-04 If clone creation is specified, the tool creates a clone of the digital source. AM-06 All visible sectors are acquired from the digital source. AM-08 All sectors acquired from the digital source are acquired accurately. AO-11 If requested, a clone is created during an acquisition of a digital source. AO-13 A clone is created using access interface DST-AI to write to the clone device. AO-14 If an unaligned clone is created, each sector written to the clone is accurately written to the same disk address on the clone that the sector occupied on the digital source. AO-17 If requested, any excess sectors on a clone destination device are not modified. AO-22 If requested, the tool calculates block hashes for a specified block size during an acquisition for each block acquired from the digital source. AO-23 If the tool logs any log significant information, the information is accurately recorded in the log file. AO-24 If the tool executes in a forensically safe execution environment, the digital source is unchanged by the acquisition process.
Tester Name:	brl
Test Host:	Paladin
Test Date:	Wed Nov 14 10:16:27 2007
Drives:	src(09-LAP) dst (F9) other (none)
Source Setup:	src hash (SHA1): < 118459903C8BB9E6D668DBFDD5D54832BE88E029 > src hash (MD5): < 602C740729A16808E42696C1D9C93C96 > 195371568 total sectors (100030242816 bytes) 12160/254/63 (max cyl/hd values) 12161/255/63 (number of cyl/hd) Model (A) serial # (5MH0KZ) This drive has a DCO of 8000001 sectors The hashes with DCO in place are: MD5: 00A81DE5822E84E9606DEF68D9D17367 SHA1: 7A247D230345EFC1A412586A83AA6AD66266D2B1
Log Highlights:	Destination setup 40188960 sectors wiped with F9 Comparision of original to clone Drive Sectors compared: 8000001 Sectors match: 8000001 Sectors differ: 0 Bytes differ: 0 Diffs range Source (8000001) has 32188959 fewer sectors than destination (40188960) Zero fill: 0 Src Byte fill (09): 0 Dst Byte fill (F9): 32188959 Other fill: 0 Other no fill: 0 Zero fill range: Src fill range: Dst fill range: 8000001-40188959 Other fill range: Other not filled range: 0 source read errors, 0 destination read errors No Log file found (da-01-xusb) Settings: error skip

Test Case DA-01-XUSB F-TALON V2.43		
	speed n/a	
Results:		
	Assertion & Expected Result	**Actual Result**
	AM-01 Source acquired using interface AI.	as expected
	AM-02 Source is type DS.	as expected
	AM-03 Execution environment is XE.	as expected
	AM-04 A clone is created.	as expected
	AM-06 All visible sectors acquired.	as expected
	AM-08 All sectors accurately acquired.	as expected
	AO-11 A clone is created during acquisition.	as expected
	AO-13 Clone created using interface AI.	as expected
	AO-14 An unaligned clone is created.	as expected
	AO-17 Excess sectors are unchanged.	as expected
	AO-22 Tool calculates hashes by block.	option not tested
	AO-23 Logged information is correct.	as expected
	AO-24 Source is unchanged by acquisition.	as expected
Analysis:	Expected results achieved	

5.2.8 DA-04

Test Case DA-04 F-TALON V2.43	
Case Summary:	DA-04 Acquire a physical device to a truncated clone.
Assertions:	AM-01 The tool uses access interface SRC-AI to access the digital source. AM-02 The tool acquires digital source DS. AM-03 The tool executes in execution environment XE. AM-04 If clone creation is specified, the tool creates a clone of the digital source. AM-06 All visible sectors are acquired from the digital source. AM-08 All sectors acquired from the digital source are acquired accurately. AO-11 If requested, a clone is created during an acquisition of a digital source. AO-13 A clone is created using access interface DST-AI to write to the clone device. AO-14 If an unaligned clone is created, each sector written to the clone is accurately written to the same disk address on the clone that the sector occupied on the digital source. AO-19 If there is insufficient space to create a complete clone, a truncated clone is created using all available sectors of the clone device. AO-20 If a truncated clone is created, the tool notifies the user. AO-22 If requested, the tool calculates block hashes for a specified block size during an acquisition for each block acquired from the digital source. AO-23 If the tool logs any log significant information, the information is accurately recorded in the log file. AO-24 If the tool executes in a forensically safe execution environment, the digital source is unchanged by the acquisition process.
Tester Name:	brl
Test Host:	Aramis
Test Date:	Thu Oct 25 02:30:54 2007
Drives:	src(41) dst (AA) other (none)
Source Setup:	src hash (SHA256): < FBF3AA21489653D880FFAE71449A9F7E8EE4F56A6C3BF58A3A3FFB13203F1B1D > src hash (SHA1): < 15CAA1A307271160D8372668BF8A03FC45A51CC9 > src hash (MD5): < 0A6A8EF78BDC14E2026710D8CCB5607C > 78125000 total sectors (40000000000 bytes) 65534/015/63 (max cyl/hd values) 65535/016/63 (number of cyl/hd) IDE disk: Model (WDC WD400BB-75JHC0) serial # (WD-WMAMC4658355) N Start LBA Length Start C/H/S End C/H/S boot Partition type 1 P 000000063 078107967 0000/001/01 1023/254/63 Boot 07 NTFS 2 P 000000000 000000000 0000/000/00 0000/000/00 00 empty entry 3 P 000000000 000000000 0000/000/00 0000/000/00 00 empty entry 4 P 000000000 000000000 0000/000/00 0000/000/00 00 empty entry 1 078107967 sectors 39991279104 bytes
Log Highlights:	Destination setup 60030432 sectors wiped with AA No Log file found (da-04) Screen message: Error Capturing Drive! Cannot fit data to target drive! Settings: error skip speed UDMA-5

Results:

Assertion & Expected Result	Actual Result
AM-01 Source acquired using interface AI.	as expected
AM-02 Source is type DS.	as expected
AM-03 Execution environment is XE.	as expected
AM-04 A clone is created.	as expected
AM-06 All visible sectors acquired.	as expected
AM-08 All sectors accurately acquired.	as expected
AO-11 A clone is created during acquisition.	as expected
AO-13 Clone created using interface AI.	as expected

Test Case DA-04 F-TALON V2.43		
	AO-14 An unaligned clone is created.	as expected
	AO-19 Truncated clone is created.	as expected
	AO-20 User notified that clone is truncated.	as expected
	AO-22 Tool calculates hashes by block.	option not tested
	AO-23 Logged information is correct.	as expected
	AO-24 Source is unchanged by acquisition.	as expected
Analysis:	Expected results achieved	

5.2.9 DA-06-ATA28

Test Case DA-06-ATA28 F-TALON V2.43	
Case Summary:	DA-06 Acquire a physical device using access interface AI to an image file.
Assertions:	AM-01 The tool uses access interface SRC-AI to access the digital source. AM-02 The tool acquires digital source DS. AM-03 The tool executes in execution environment XE. AM-05 If image file creation is specified, the tool creates an image file on file system type FS. AM-06 All visible sectors are acquired from the digital source. AM-08 All sectors acquired from the digital source are acquired accurately. AO-01 If the tool creates an image file, the data represented by the image file is the same as the data acquired by the tool. AO-05 If the tool creates a multi-file image of a requested size then all the individual files shall be no larger than the requested size. AO-22 If requested, the tool calculates block hashes for a specified block size during an acquisition for each block acquired from the digital source. AO-23 If the tool logs any log significant information, the information is accurately recorded in the log file. AO-24 If the tool executes in a forensically safe execution environment, the digital source is unchanged by the acquisition process.
Tester Name:	brl
Test Host:	Athos
Test Date:	Wed Oct 31 12:30:07 2007
Drives:	src(41) dst (none) other (22-SATA)

Source Setup:	src hash (SHA256): <
	FBF3AA21489653D880FFAE71449A9F7E8EE4F56A6C3BF58A3A3FFB13203F1B1D >
	src hash (SHA1): < 15CAA1A307271160D8372668BF8A03FC45A51CC9 >
	src hash (MD5): < 0A6A8EF78BDC14E2026710D8CCB5607C >
	
	Reference MD5 hashes, Win size: 666238976 (bytes)
	    1 0 - 666238975 46E843537F40B1931C2859B4E36DA015 -
	    2 666238976 - 1332477951 34CA5E7FD7A3EF769C2C80FE3338D9D2 -
	    3 1332477952 - 1998716927 DC8EF08B34A158DCD492A992AEC634BB -
	       . . .
	   59 38641860608 - 39308099583 646D67FA5B92F92C5F325592D66672A3 -
	   60 39308099584 - 39974338559 1DCCFCD2AFA92A1D933D539A13A9EDAA -
	   61 39974338560 - 40640577535 EE8E6AA702E441CD341BD9B109E0C7ED -
	78125000 total sectors (40000000000 bytes)
	65534/015/63 (max cyl/hd values)
	65535/016/63 (number of cyl/hd)
	IDE disk: Model (WDC WD400BB-75JHC0) serial # (WD-WMAMC4658355)
	N Start LBA Length Start C/H/S End C/H/S boot Partition type
	1 P 000000063 078107967 0000/001/01 1023/254/63 Boot 07 NTFS
	2 P 000000000 000000000 0000/000/00 0000/000/00 00 empty entry
	3 P 000000000 000000000 0000/000/00 0000/000/00 00 empty entry
	4 P 000000000 000000000 0000/000/00 0000/000/00 00 empty entry
	1 078107967 sectors 39991279104 bytes

Log Highlights:	***** FORENSIC TALON Serial No.: 15881 Software: V2.43 *****
	                 SESSION SETTINGS
	   Operating Mode: DD Img(650M) Address Mode: LBA
	   Verify : MD5-File Speed : PIO-AUTO
	   Connection : Direct
	************************ SOURCE DRIVE ************************
	               Physical Characteristics
	   Drive Model: WDC WD400BB-75JHC0
	     Serial: WD-WMAMC4658355
	    Cylinders Heads Sectors Total Sectors Drive Size
	     77504 16 63 78125000 37.3 GB
	********************** DESTINATION DRIVE **********************
	               Physical Characteristics
	   Drive Model: ST380013AS
	     Serial: 5JVCQ731
	    Cylinders Heads Sectors Total Sectors Drive Size
	    155061 16 63 156301488 74.5 GB

```
              Skipped Sectors: 0     Recovered Sectors: 0
       Block Hashes
        06ATA28.001: From:0, To:1332521, Size:1301248, MD5 Value:
           46E843537F40B1931C2859B4E36DA015
        06ATA28.002: From:1301248, To:2633769, Size:1301248, MD5 Value:
           34CA5E7FD7A3EF769C2C80FE3338D9D2
        06ATA28.003: From:2602496, To:3935017, Size:1301248, MD5 Value:
           DC8EF08B34A158DCD492A992AEC634BB
           . . .
        06ATA28.059: From:75472384, To:76804905, Size:1301248, MD5 Value:
           646D67FA5B92F92C5F325592D66672A3
        06ATA28.060: From:76773632, To:78106153, Size:1301248, MD5 Value:
           1DCCFCD2AFA92A1D933D539A13A9EDAA
        06ATA28.061: From:78074880, To:79407401, Size:50120, MD5 Value:
           EE8E6AA702E441CD341BD9B109E0C7ED
       Settings: error skip
       speed PIO-AUTO
```

Results:

Assertion & Expected Result	Actual Result
AM-01 Source acquired using interface AI.	as expected
AM-02 Source is type DS.	as expected
AM-03 Execution environment is XE.	as expected
AM-05 An image is created on file system type FS.	as expected
AM-06 All visible sectors acquired.	as expected
AM-08 All sectors accurately acquired.	as expected
AO-01 Image file is complete and accurate.	as expected
AO-05 Multifile image created.	as expected
AO-22 Tool calculates hashes by block.	as expected
AO-23 Logged information is correct.	as expected
AO-24 Source is unchanged by acquisition.	as expected

Analysis: Expected results achieved

5.2.10   DA-06-ATA48

Test Case DA-06-ATA48 F-TALON V2.43	
Case Summary:	DA-06 Acquire a physical device using access interface AI to an image file.
Assertions:	AM-01 The tool uses access interface SRC-AI to access the digital source. AM-02 The tool acquires digital source DS. AM-03 The tool executes in execution environment XE. AM-05 If image file creation is specified, the tool creates an image file on file system type FS. AM-06 All visible sectors are acquired from the digital source. AM-08 All sectors acquired from the digital source are acquired accurately. AO-01 If the tool creates an image file, the data represented by the image file is the same as the data acquired by the tool. AO-05 If the tool creates a multi-file image of a requested size then all the individual files shall be no larger than the requested size. AO-22 If requested, the tool calculates block hashes for a specified block size during an acquisition for each block acquired from the digital source. AO-23 If the tool logs any log significant information, the information is accurately recorded in the log file. AO-24 If the tool executes in a forensically safe execution environment, the digital source is unchanged by the acquisition process.
Tester Name:	brl
Test Host:	Aramis
Test Date:	Fri Oct 26 00:41:27 2007
Drives:	src(4C) dst (none) other (28-IDE)

Source Setup:	src hash (SHA1): < 8FF620D2BEDCCAFE8412EDAAD56C8554F872EFBF >
	src hash (MD5): < D10F763B56D4CEBA2D1311C61F9FB382 >
	
	Reference MD5 hashes, Win size: 3997433856 (bytes)
	   1 0 - 3997433855 A24BA8F8CED07E07515A6FF70C21DC83 -
	   2 3997433856 - 7994867711 5A3641B34D935EE37158329A81BA7D34 -
	   3 7994867712 - 11992301567 296AB048E52814A74B21ECE0DC7F7AC3 -
	      . . .
	   49 191876825088 - 195874258943 C3D90AF2D73937250E97439F82EBA0EC -
	   50 195874258944 - 199871692799 DFEC8704F5C94CB4674C7B29762009AF -
	   51 199871692800 - 200049647615 A7FD8741B79971412099A34AA5D027A4 -
	390721968 total sectors (200049647616 bytes)
	24320/254/63 (max cyl/hd values)
	24321/255/63 (number of cyl/hd)
	IDE disk: Model (WDC WD2000JB-00KFA0) serial # (WD-WMAMR1031111)
	N Start LBA Length Start C/H/S End C/H/S boot Partition type
	1 P 000000063 390700737 0000/001/01 1023/254/63 Boot 07 NTFS
	2 P 000000000 000000000 0000/000/00 0000/000/00 00 empty entry
	3 P 000000000 000000000 0000/000/00 0000/000/00 00 empty entry
	4 P 000000000 000000000 0000/000/00 0000/000/00 00 empty entry
	1 390700737 sectors 200038777344 bytes

Log Highlights:	***** FORENSIC TALON Serial No.: 15881 Software: V2.43 *****
	                    SESSION SETTINGS
	    Operating Mode: DD Img(4GB) Address Mode: LBA
	    Verify : MD5-File Speed : UDMA-4
	    Connection : Direct
	          AN EXACT DD IMAGE FILE COPY OF THE SUSPECT DRIVE HAS
	          BEEN SUCCESSFULLY EXECUTED ON THE EVIDENCE DRIVE!
	************************ SOURCE DRIVE ************************
	                  Physical Characteristics
	    Drive Model: WDC WD2000JB-00KFA0
	       Serial: WD-WMAMR1031111
	    Cylinders Heads Sectors Total Sectors Drive Size
	       387621 16 63 390721968 186.3 GB
	********************** DESTINATION DRIVE **********************
	                  Physical Characteristics
	    Drive Model: WDC WD2500JB-00GVC0
	       Serial: WD-WCAL78181051
	    Cylinders Heads Sectors Total Sectors Drive Size
	       484521 16 63 488397168 232.9 GB
	       Skipped Sectors: 0 Recovered Sectors: 0

Block Hashes
06ATA48.001: From:0, To:7926229, Size:7807488, MD5 Value:
  A24BA8F8CED07E07515A6FF70C21DC83
06ATA48.002: From:7807488, To:15733717, Size:7807488, MD5 Value:
  5A3641B34D935EE37158329A81BA7D34
06ATA48.003: From:15614976, To:23541205, Size:7807488, MD5 Value:
  296AB048E52814A74B21ECE0DC7F7AC3
  . . .
06ATA48.049: From:374759424, To:382685653, Size:7807488, MD5 Value:
  C3D90AF2D73937250E97439F82EBA0EC
06ATA48.050: From:382566912, To:390493141, Size:7807488, MD5 Value:
  DFEC8704F5C94CB4674C7B29762009AF
06ATA48.051: From:390374400, To:398300629, Size:347568, MD5 Value:
  A7FD8741B79971412099A34AA5D027A4
Settings: error skip
speed UDMA-5

Results:

Assertion & Expected Result	Actual Result
AM-01 Source acquired using interface AI.	as expected
AM-02 Source is type DS.	as expected
AM-03 Execution environment is XE.	as expected
AM-05 An image is created on file system type FS.	as expected
AM-06 All visible sectors acquired.	as expected
AM-08 All sectors accurately acquired.	as expected
AO-01 Image file is complete and accurate.	as expected
AO-05 Multifile image created.	as expected
AO-22 Tool calculates hashes by block.	as expected
AO-23 Logged information is correct.	as expected
AO-24 Source is unchanged by acquisition.	as expected

Analysis: Expected results achieved

5.2.11   DA-06-SATA28

Test Case DA-06-SATA28 F-TALON V2.43	
Case Summary:	DA-06 Acquire a physical device using access interface AI to an image file.
Assertions:	AM-01 The tool uses access interface SRC-AI to access the digital source.
	AM-02 The tool acquires digital source DS.
	AM-03 The tool executes in execution environment XE.
	AM-05 If image file creation is specified, the tool creates an image file on file system type FS.
	AM-06 All visible sectors are acquired from the digital source.
	AM-08 All sectors acquired from the digital source are acquired accurately.
	AO-01 If the tool creates an image file, the data represented by the image file is the same as the data acquired by the tool.
	AO-05 If the tool creates a multi-file image of a requested size then all the individual files shall be no larger than the requested size.
	AO-22 If requested, the tool calculates block hashes for a specified block size during an acquisition for each block acquired from the digital source.
	AO-23 If the tool logs any log significant information, the information is accurately recorded in the log file.
	AO-24 If the tool executes in a forensically safe execution environment, the digital source is unchanged by the acquisition process.
Tester Name:	brl
Test Host:	Athos
Test Date:	Tue Oct 30 14:53:17 2007
Drives:	src(07-SATA) dst (none) other (13-IDE)
Source Setup:	src hash (SHA1): < 655E9BDDB36A3F9C5C4CC8BF32B8C5B41AF9F52E >
	src hash (MD5): < 2EAF712DAD80F66E30DEA00365B4579B >
	Reference SHA256 hashes, Win size: 3903744 (sectors)
	1 0 - 3903743
	043AA89C79D5D22715C1E0B28AB86807DC11DE46C1781DECC0AB98E85BF59E40
	2 3903744 - 7807487
	86C2063F55FA5BDCC0379AF77A73E840909F79F51158CC3523813A57109CB65F
	3 7807488 - 11711231
	C4876353FCEB0814F8A5B522E67B474113F0E1ECC64F6992662A11AA58138DCC
	. . .
	39 148342272 - 152246015
	1830C6D075DFEA26B8855B81DC02676B795E8D9F179C99F0ACCC4B7F07EDF847
	40 152246016 - 156149759
	C7E9434D4443928C6A2BBF388CB65DA3CC3F3738459764FF1ABC639E3863049A
	41 156149760 - 160053503
	07AAA567626F5FF3B4375F1D43F308790209492757B65388B27743819BC8F9DF
	156301488 total sectors (80026361856 bytes)
	Model (WDC WD800JD-32HK) serial # (WD-WMAJ91510044)
	N Start LBA Length Start C/H/S End C/H/S boot Partition type
	1 P 000000063 156280257 0000/001/01 1023/254/63 Boot 07 NTFS
	2 P 000000000 000000000 0000/000/00 0000/000/00 00 empty entry
	3 P 000000000 000000000 0000/000/00 0000/000/00 00 empty entry
	4 P 000000000 000000000 0000/000/00 0000/000/00 00 empty entry
	1 156280257 sectors 80015491584 bytes
Log Highlights:	***** FORENSIC TALON Serial No.: 15881 Software: V2.43 *****
	SESSION SETTINGS
	Operating Mode: DD Img(2GB) Address Mode: LBA
	Verify : SHA-Fil+V Speed : UDMA-5
	Connection : Direct
	AN EXACT DD IMAGE FILE COPY OF THE SUSPECT DRIVE HAS
	BEEN SUCCESSFULLY EXECUTED ON THE EVIDENCE DRIVE!
	************************* SOURCE DRIVE ************************
	Physical Characteristics
	Drive Model: WDC WD800JD-32HKA0
	Serial: WD-WMAJ91510044
	Cylinders Heads Sectors Total Sectors Drive Size
	155061 16 63 156301488 74.5 GB
	*********************** DESTINATION DRIVE **********************
	Physical Characteristics

```
Test Case DA-06-SATA28 F-TALON V2.43
             Drive Model: MAXTOR STM3120814A
                   Serial: 5LS6PD2S
             Cylinders    Heads    Sectors    Total Sectors    Drive Size
              232581       16        63         234441648       111.8 GB
             Skipped Sectors: 0     Recovered Sectors: 0
          Block Hashes
          06SATA28.001: From:0, To:4017967, Size:3903744, SHA-256:
             043AA89C79D5D22715C1E0B28AB86807DC11DE46C1781DECC0AB98E85BF59E40
          06SATA28.002: From:3903744, To:7921711, Size:3903744, SHA-256:
             86C2063F55FA5BDCC0379AF77A73E840909F79F51158CC3523813A57109CB65F
          06SATA28.003: From:7807488, To:11825455, Size:3903744, SHA-256:
             C4876353FCEB0814F8A5B522E67B474113F0E1ECC64F6992662A11AA58138DCC
             . . .
          06SATA28.039: From:148342272, To:152360239, Size:3903744, SHA-256:
             1830C6D075DFEA26B8855B81DC02676B795E8D9F179C99F0ACCC4B7F07EDF847
          06SATA28.040: From:152246016, To:156263983, Size:3903744, SHA-256:
             C7E9434D4443928C6A2BBF388CB65DA3CC3F3738459764FF1ABC639E3863049A
          06SATA28.041: From:156149760, To:160167727, Size:151728, SHA-256:
             07AAA567626F5FF3B4375F1D43F308790209492757B65388B27743819BC8F9DF
          Settings: error skip
          speed UDMA-5
```

Results:

Assertion & Expected Result	Actual Result
AM-01 Source acquired using interface AI.	as expected
AM-02 Source is type DS.	as expected
AM-03 Execution environment is XE.	as expected
AM-05 An image is created on file system type FS.	as expected
AM-06 All visible sectors acquired.	as expected
AM-08 All sectors accurately acquired.	as expected
AO-01 Image file is complete and accurate.	as expected
AO-05 Multifile image created.	as expected
AO-22 Tool calculates hashes by block.	as expected
AO-23 Logged information is correct.	as expected
AO-24 Source is unchanged by acquisition.	as expected

Analysis: Expected results achieved

5.2.12   DA-06-SATA48

Test Case DA-06-SATA48 F-TALON V2.43	
Case Summary:	DA-06 Acquire a physical device using access interface AI to an image file.
Assertions:	AM-01 The tool uses access interface SRC-AI to access the digital source. AM-02 The tool acquires digital source DS. AM-03 The tool executes in execution environment XE. AM-05 If image file creation is specified, the tool creates an image file on file system type FS. AM-06 All visible sectors are acquired from the digital source. AM-08 All sectors acquired from the digital source are acquired accurately. AO-01 If the tool creates an image file, the data represented by the image file is the same as the data acquired by the tool. AO-05 If the tool creates a multi-file image of a requested size then all the individual files shall be no larger than the requested size. AO-22 If requested, the tool calculates block hashes for a specified block size during an acquisition for each block acquired from the digital source. AO-23 If the tool logs any log significant information, the information is accurately recorded in the log file. AO-24 If the tool executes in a forensically safe execution environment, the digital source is unchanged by the acquisition process.
Tester Name:	brl
Test Host:	Athos
Test Date:	Mon Oct 29 15:40:17 2007
Drives:	src(0D-SATA) dst (none) other (1D-SATA)
Source Setup:	src hash (SHA1): < BAAD80E8781E55F2E3EF528CA73BD41D228C1377 > src hash (MD5): < 1FA7C3CBE60EB9E89863DED2411E40C9 > 488397168 total sectors (250059350016 bytes) 30400/254/63 (max cyl/hd values) 30401/255/63 (number of cyl/hd) Model (WDC WD2500JD-22F) serial # (WD-WMAEH2678216) N Start LBA Length Start C/H/S End C/H/S boot Partition type 1 P 000000063 488375937 0000/001/01 1023/254/63 Boot 07 NTFS 2 P 000000000 000000000 0000/000/00 0000/000/00 00 empty entry 3 P 000000000 000000000 0000/000/00 0000/000/00 00 empty entry 4 P 000000000 000000000 0000/000/00 0000/000/00 00 empty entry 1 488375937 sectors 250048479744 bytes

Log Highlights:	***** FORENSIC TALON Serial No.: 15881 Software: V2.43 *****
	                        SESSION SETTINGS
	Operating Mode: DD Img(650M) Address Mode: LBA
	Verify : MD5-Disk Speed : UDMA-4
	Connection : Direct
	        AN EXACT DD IMAGE FILE COPY OF THE SUSPECT DRIVE HAS
	        BEEN SUCCESSFULLY EXECUTED ON THE EVIDENCE DRIVE!
	************************ SOURCE DRIVE ************************
	                    Physical Characteristics
	Drive Model: WDC WD2500JD-22FYB0
	    Serial: WD-WMAEH2678216
	    Cylinders Heads Sectors Total Sectors Drive Size
	     484521 16 63 488397168 232.9 GB
	********************** DESTINATION DRIVE **********************
	                    Physical Characteristics
	Drive Model: ST3320620AS
	    Serial: 5QF3YS2E
	    Cylinders Heads Sectors Total Sectors Drive Size
	     620181 16 63 625142448 298.1 GB
	    Skipped Sectors: 0 Recovered Sectors: 0
	* Source Drive From:0, To:488397167, Size:488397168, MD5 Value:
	Acquisition Hash
	 Source Drive From:0, To:488397167, Size:488397168, MD5 Value:
	  1FA7C3CBE60EB9E89863DED2411E40C9
	
	Settings: error skip
	speed UDMA-5

Results:	

Test Case DA-06-SATA48 F-TALON V2.43		
	Assertion & Expected Result	**Actual Result**
	AM-01 Source acquired using interface AI.	as expected
	AM-02 Source is type DS.	as expected
	AM-03 Execution environment is XE.	as expected
	AM-05 An image is created on file system type FS.	as expected
	AM-06 All visible sectors acquired.	as expected
	AM-08 All sectors accurately acquired.	as expected
	AO-01 Image file is complete and accurate.	as expected
	AO-05 Multifile image created.	as expected
	AO-22 Tool calculates hashes by block.	option not tested
	AO-23 Logged information is correct.	as expected
	AO-24 Source is unchanged by acquisition.	as expected
Analysis:	Expected results achieved	

5.2.13 DA-06-USB

Test Case DA-06-USB F-TALON V2.43	
Case Summary:	DA-06 Acquire a physical device using access interface AI to an image file.
Assertions:	AM-01 The tool uses access interface SRC-AI to access the digital source. AM-02 The tool acquires digital source DS. AM-03 The tool executes in execution environment XE. AM-05 If image file creation is specified, the tool creates an image file on file system type FS. AM-06 All visible sectors are acquired from the digital source. AM-08 All sectors acquired from the digital source are acquired accurately. AO-01 If the tool creates an image file, the data represented by the image file is the same as the data acquired by the tool. AO-05 If the tool creates a multi-file image of a requested size then all the individual files shall be no larger than the requested size. AO-22 If requested, the tool calculates block hashes for a specified block size during an acquisition for each block acquired from the digital source. AO-23 If the tool logs any log significant information, the information is accurately recorded in the log file. AO-24 If the tool executes in a forensically safe execution environment, the digital source is unchanged by the acquisition process.
Tester Name:	brl
Test Host:	Athos
Test Date:	Wed Oct 31 14:06:34 2007
Drives:	src(D5-THUMB) dst (none) other (5A)
Source Setup:	src hash (SHA1): < D68520EF74A336E49DCCF83815B7B08FDC53E38A > src hash (MD5): < C843593624B2B3B878596D8760B19954 > 505856 total sectors (258998272 bytes) Model (usb2.0Flash Disk) serial # () N Start LBA Length Start C/H/S End C/H/S boot Partition type 1 P 778135908 1141509631 0357/116/40 0357/032/45 Boot 72 other 2 P 168689522 1936028240 0288/115/43 0367/114/50 Boot 65 other 3 P 1869881465 1936028192 0366/032/33 0357/032/43 Boot 79 other 4 P 2885681152 000055499 0372/097/50 0000/010/00 Boot 0D other 1 1141509631 sectors 584452931072 bytes 2 1936028240 sectors 991246458880 bytes 3 1936028192 sectors 991246434304 bytes 4 000055499 sectors 28415488 bytes

Log Highlights:	***** FORENSIC TALON Serial No.: 15881 Software: V2.43 *****
	                     SESSION SETTINGS
	   Operating Mode: DD Img(4GB) Address Mode: LBA
	   Verify : MD5-Disk Speed : PIO-AUTO
	   Connection : Direct
	          AN EXACT DD IMAGE FILE COPY OF THE SUSPECT DRIVE HAS
	           BEEN SUCCESSFULLY EXECUTED ON THE EVIDENCE DRIVE!
	************************ SOURCE DRIVE *************************
	                  Physical Characteristics
	   Drive Model: CRUCIAL usb2.0Flash Disk
	        Serial:
	     Cylinders Heads Sectors Total Sectors Drive Size
	       501 16 63 505856 0.2 GB
	********************** DESTINATION DRIVE **********************
	                  Physical Characteristics
	   Drive Model: IBM-DTTA-350640
	        Serial: WD0WDF99294
	     Cylinders Heads Sectors Total Sectors Drive Size
	      13431 15 63 12692736 6.1 GB
	        Skipped Sectors: 0 Recovered Sectors: 0
	* Source Drive From:0, To:505855, Size:505856, MD5 Value:
	Acquisition Hash
	 Source Drive From:0, To:505855, Size:505856, MD5 Value:
	   C843593624B2B3B878596D8760B19954
	
	Settings: error skip
	speed PIO-AUTO

Test Case DA-06-USB F-TALON V2.43	
Results:	

Assertion & Expected Result	Actual Result
AM-01 Source acquired using interface AI.	as expected
AM-02 Source is type DS.	as expected
AM-03 Execution environment is XE.	as expected
AM-05 An image is created on file system type FS.	as expected
AM-06 All visible sectors acquired.	as expected
AM-08 All sectors accurately acquired.	as expected
AO-01 Image file is complete and accurate.	as expected
AO-05 Multifile image created.	as expected
AO-22 Tool calculates hashes by block.	option not tested
AO-23 Logged information is correct.	as expected
AO-24 Source is unchanged by acquisition.	as expected

Analysis:	Expected results achieved

5.2.14   DA-07-CF

Test Case DA-07-CF F-TALON V2.43	
Case Summary:	DA-07 Acquire a digital source of type DS to an image file.
Assertions:	AM-01 The tool uses access interface SRC-AI to access the digital source. AM-02 The tool acquires digital source DS. AM-03 The tool executes in execution environment XE. AM-05 If image file creation is specified, the tool creates an image file on file system type FS. AM-06 All visible sectors are acquired from the digital source. AM-08 All sectors acquired from the digital source are acquired accurately. AO-01 If the tool creates an image file, the data represented by the image file is the same as the data acquired by the tool. AO-05 If the tool creates a multi-file image of a requested size then all the individual files shall be no larger than the requested size. AO-22 If requested, the tool calculates block hashes for a specified block size during an acquisition for each block acquired from the digital source. AO-23 If the tool logs any log significant information, the information is accurately recorded in the log file. AO-24 If the tool executes in a forensically safe execution environment, the digital source is unchanged by the acquisition process.
Tester Name:	brl
Test Host:	Paladin
Test Date:	Wed Oct 31 15:04:43 2007
Drives:	src(C1-CF) dst (none) other (5A)
Source Setup:	src hash (SHA256): < C7CF0218222DF80D5316511D6814266C7FA507C13F795AD3D323BB73C1590D80 > src hash (SHA1): < 5B8235178DF99FA307430C088F81746606638A0B > src hash (MD5): < 776DF8B4D2589E21DEBCF589EDC16D78 > 503808 total sectors (257949696 bytes) Model (CF) serial # () N Start LBA Length Start C/H/S End C/H/S boot Partition type 1 P 778135908 1141509631 0357/116/40 0357/032/45 Boot 72 other 2 P 168689522 1936028240 0288/115/43 0367/114/50 Boot 65 other 3 P 1869881465 1936028192 0366/032/33 0357/032/43 Boot 79 other 4 P 2885681152 000055499 0372/097/50 0000/010/00 Boot 0D other 1 1141509631 sectors 584452931072 bytes 2 1936028240 sectors 991246458880 bytes 3 1936028192 sectors 991246434304 bytes 4 000055499 sectors 28415488 bytes

Log Highlights:	***** FORENSIC TALON Serial No.: 15881 Software: V2.43 *****
	                    SESSION SETTINGS
	Operating Mode: DD Img(650M) Address Mode: LBA
	Verify : MD5-File Speed : PIO-AUTO
	Connection : Direct
	     AN EXACT DD IMAGE FILE COPY OF THE SUSPECT DRIVE HAS
	      BEEN SUCCESSFULLY EXECUTED ON THE EVIDENCE DRIVE!
	************************* SOURCE DRIVE *************************
	             Physical Characteristics
	Drive Model: ICSI CF Card CF
	   Serial:
	  Cylinders Heads Sectors Total Sectors Drive Size
	    499 16 63 503808 0.2 GB
	********************* DESTINATION DRIVE *********************
	             Physical Characteristics
	Drive Model: IBM-DTTA-350640
	   Serial: WD0WDF99294
	  Cylinders Heads Sectors Total Sectors Drive Size
	  13431 15 63 12692736 6.1 GB
	    Skipped Sectors: 0 Recovered Sectors: 0
	* 07CF.001: From:0, To:1325331, Size:503808, MD5 Value:
	Acquisition Hash
	 07CF.001: From:0, To:1325331, Size:503808, MD5 Value:
	  776DF8B4D2589E21DEBCF589EDC16D78

Test Case DA-07-CF F-TALON V2.43	
	Settings: error skip speed PIO-AUTO
Results:	

Assertion & Expected Result	Actual Result
AM-01 Source acquired using interface AI.	as expected
AM-02 Source is type DS.	as expected
AM-03 Execution environment is XE.	as expected
AM-05 An image is created on file system type FS.	as expected
AM-06 All visible sectors acquired.	as expected
AM-08 All sectors accurately acquired.	as expected
AO-01 Image file is complete and accurate.	as expected
AO-05 Multifile image created.	as expected
AO-22 Tool calculates hashes by block.	option not tested
AO-23 Logged information is correct.	as expected
AO-24 Source is unchanged by acquisition.	as expected

Analysis:	Expected results achieved

5.2.15 DA-08-ATA28

Test Case DA-08-ATA28 F-TALON V2.43	
Case Summary:	DA-08 Acquire a physical drive with hidden sectors to an image file.
Assertions:	AM-01 The tool uses access interface SRC-AI to access the digital source. AM-02 The tool acquires digital source DS. AM-03 The tool executes in execution environment XE. AM-05 If image file creation is specified, the tool creates an image file on file system type FS. AM-06 All visible sectors are acquired from the digital source. AM-07 All hidden sectors are acquired from the digital source. AM-08 All sectors acquired from the digital source are acquired accurately. AO-01 If the tool creates an image file, the data represented by the image file is the same as the data acquired by the tool. AO-05 If the tool creates a multi-file image of a requested size then all the individual files shall be no larger than the requested size. AO-22 If requested, the tool calculates block hashes for a specified block size during an acquisition for each block acquired from the digital source. AO-23 If the tool logs any log significant information, the information is accurately recorded in the log file. AO-24 If the tool executes in a forensically safe execution environment, the digital source is unchanged by the acquisition process.
Tester Name:	brl
Test Host:	Paladin
Test Date:	Wed Oct 31 16:00:24 2007
Drives:	src(42) dst (none) other (23-IDE)

Source Setup:	src hash (SHA1): < 5A75399023056E0EB905082B35F8FAA1DB049229 > src hash (MD5): < F4B9AAB24554EEEB2A962BDA554A9252 >
	
	Reference MD5 hashes, Win size: 1301248 (sectors)
	    1 0 - 1301247 4C09659BDFF6385AEC8430C6748DE2CE -
	    2 1301248 - 2602495 D1737C33CBE394D17EFA80CB1576D498 -
	    3 2602496 - 3903743 35300547B2FE971755257FDA3FD76C77 -
	    . . .
	   59 75472384 - 76773631 6541BC90D2D418C8451A935DB6539206 -
	   60 76773632 - 78074879 E6F50867FE12B5A3D74383E6C17888AC -
	   61 78074880 - 79376127 4D92ABF2A131DF5A5C3D0DFB318DDE27 -
	78165360 total sectors (40020664320 bytes)
	65534/015/63 (max cyl/hd values)
	65535/016/63 (number of cyl/hd)
	IDE disk: Model (WDC WD400JB-00JJC0) serial # (WD-WCAMA3958512)
	 N Start LBA Length Start C/H/S End C/H/S boot Partition type
	 1 P 000000063 070348572 0000/001/01 1023/254/63 Boot 07 NTFS
	 2 P 000000000 000000000 0000/000/00 0000/000/00 00 empty entry
	 3 P 000000000 000000000 0000/000/00 0000/000/00 00 empty entry
	 4 P 000000000 000000000 0000/000/00 0000/000/00 00 empty entry
	1 070348572 sectors 36018468864 bytes
	
	HPA created
	BIOS, XBIOS and Direct disk geometry Reporter (BXDR)
	BXDR 128 /S70000000 /P /fbxdrlog.txt
	Setting Maximum Addressable Sector to 70000000
	MAS now set to 70000000
	
	Hashes with HPA in place
	md5:9BF3C3DEADE47056A1DDC073C5F6B2E2
	sha1:D76F909482B00767B62C295CADE202F92E61CD2E

Log Highlights:	***** FORENSIC TALON Serial No.: 15881 Software: V2.43 *****
	                     SESSION SETTINGS
	Operating Mode: DD Img(650M) Address Mode: LBA
	Verify : MD5-File Speed : UDMA-4
	Connection : Direct
	         AN EXACT DD IMAGE FILE COPY OF THE SUSPECT DRIVE HAS
	        BEEN SUCCESSFULLY EXECUTED ON THE EVIDENCE DRIVE!
	************************ SOURCE DRIVE ************************
	                 Physical Characteristics

```
              Drive Model: WDC WD400JB-00JJC0
                   Serial: WD-WCAMA3958512
            Cylinders    Heads    Sectors    Total Sectors    Drive Size
              77545       16        63         78165360          37.3 GB
            ***********************  DESTINATION DRIVE  **********************
                           Physical Characteristics
              Drive Model: Maxtor 6L100P0
                   Serial: L26YGVQG
            Cylinders    Heads    Sectors    Total Sectors    Drive Size
             194259       16        63        195813072          93.4 GB
              Skipped Sectors: 0      Recovered Sectors: 0
       Block Hashes
       08ATA28.001: From:0, To:1342165, Size:1301248, MD5 Value:
            4C09659BDFF6385AEC8430C6748DE2CE
       08ATA28.002: From:1301248, To:2643413, Size:1301248, MD5 Value:
            D1737C33CBE394D17EFA80CB1576D498
       08ATA28.003: From:2602496, To:3944661, Size:1301248, MD5 Value:
            35300547B2FE971755257FDA3FD76C77
            . . .
       08ATA28.059: From:75472384, To:76814549, Size:1301248, MD5 Value:
            6541BC90D2D418C8451A935DB6539206
       08ATA28.060: From:76773632, To:78115797, Size:1301248, MD5 Value:
            E6F50867FE12B5A3D74383E6C17888AC
       08ATA28.061: From:78074880, To:79417045, Size:90480, MD5 Value:
            4D92ABF2A131DF5A5C3D0DFB318DDE27
       Settings: error skip
       speed UDMA-5
```

Results:		

Assertion & Expected Result	Actual Result
AM-01 Source acquired using interface AI.	as expected
AM-02 Source is type DS.	as expected
AM-03 Execution environment is XE.	as expected
AM-05 An image is created on file system type FS.	as expected
AM-06 All visible sectors acquired.	as expected
AM-07 All hidden sectors acquired.	as expected
AM-08 All sectors accurately acquired.	as expected
AO-01 Image file is complete and accurate.	as expected
AO-05 Multifile image created.	as expected
AO-22 Tool calculates hashes by block.	as expected
AO-23 Logged information is correct.	as expected
AO-24 Source is unchanged by acquisition.	as expected

Analysis:	Expected results achieved

5.2.16 DA-08-ATA48

Test Case DA-08-ATA48 F-TALON V2.43	
Case Summary:	DA-08 Acquire a physical drive with hidden sectors to an image file.
Assertions:	AM-01 The tool uses access interface SRC-AI to access the digital source. AM-02 The tool acquires digital source DS. AM-03 The tool executes in execution environment XE. AM-05 If image file creation is specified, the tool creates an image file on file system type FS. AM-06 All visible sectors are acquired from the digital source. AM-07 All hidden sectors are acquired from the digital source. AM-08 All sectors acquired from the digital source are acquired accurately. AO-01 If the tool creates an image file, the data represented by the image file is the same as the data acquired by the tool. AO-05 If the tool creates a multi-file image of a requested size then all the individual files shall be no larger than the requested size. AO-22 If requested, the tool calculates block hashes for a specified block size during an acquisition for each block acquired from the digital source. AO-23 If the tool logs any log significant information, the information is accurately recorded in the log file. AO-24 If the tool executes in a forensically safe execution environment, the digital source is unchanged by the acquisition process.
Tester Name:	brl
Test Host:	Athos
Test Date:	Thu Nov 1 10:39:58 2007
Drives:	src(4B) dst (none) other (28-IDE)

Source Setup:	src hash (SHA1): < F409920836FED76DBB60DEEEF467A6DDED5BF48E > src hash (MD5): < B5641B5A594912B4D60518304B1DE698 >
	
	Reference MD5 hashes, Win size: 7807488 (sectors)
	    1 0 - 7807487 E0BE648B0DCD8408BB651049ED08AF2C -
	    2 7807488 - 15614975 EF98DB35796126ABBC04412589FB7932 -
	    3 15614976 - 23422463 C8CFFAC6AB449242BD80E98F1F656FDA -
	    . . .
	   49 374759424 - 382566911 EDE9FDEACC276A2B28900691C92B0DB9 -
	   50 382566912 - 390374399 3175264A9003C5D980DDEB823767DFE6 -
	   51 390374400 - 398181887 D881EE19EA1A118FE1A53AD2422AE033 -
	390721968 total sectors (200049647616 bytes)
	24320/254/63 (max cyl/hd values)
	24321/255/63 (number of cyl/hd)
	IDE disk: Model (WDC WD2000JB-00GVC0) serial # (WD-WCAL78252964)
	N Start LBA Length Start C/H/S End C/H/S boot Partition type
	1 P 000000063 351646722 0000/001/01 1023/254/63 Boot 07 NTFS
	2 P 000000000 000000000 0000/000/00 0000/000/00 00 empty entry
	3 P 000000000 000000000 0000/000/00 0000/000/00 00 empty entry
	4 P 000000000 000000000 0000/000/00 0000/000/00 00 empty entry
	1 351646722 sectors 180043121664 bytes
	
	HPA created
	BIOS, XBIOS and Direct disk geometry Reporter (BXDR)
	BXDR 128 /S351000000 /P /fHPA.TXT
	Setting Maximum Addressable Sector to 351000000
	MAS now set to 351000000
	
	Hashes with HPA in place
	md5:6BAFEFC000470C126434D933429C879B
	sha1:2D50DBD82CD3DA90A6E5BF13B2B40808C40998A1

Log Highlights:	***** FORENSIC TALON Serial No.: 15881 Software: V2.43 *****
	                  SESSION SETTINGS
	  Operating Mode: DD Img(4GB) Address Mode: LBA
	  Verify : MD5-File Speed : UDMA-4
	  Connection : Direct
	        AN EXACT DD IMAGE FILE COPY OF THE SUSPECT DRIVE HAS
	         BEEN SUCCESSFULLY EXECUTED ON THE EVIDENCE DRIVE!
	  ************************* SOURCE DRIVE *************************
	                Physical Characteristics

```
              Drive Model: WDC WD2000JB-00GVC0
                 Serial: WD-WCAL78252964
         Cylinders    Heads    Sectors    Total Sectors    Drive Size
           387621      16        63        390721968        186.3 GB
         ***********************  DESTINATION DRIVE  ***********************
                      Physical Characteristics
              Drive Model: WDC WD2500JB-00GVC0
                 Serial: WD-WCAL78181051
         Cylinders    Heads    Sectors    Total Sectors    Drive Size
           484521      16        63        488397168        232.9 GB
              Skipped Sectors: 0     Recovered Sectors: 0
    Block Hashes
    08ATA48.001: From:0, To:7926229, Size:7807488, MD5 Value:
       E0BE648B0DCD8408BB651049ED08AF2C
    08ATA48.002: From:7807488, To:15733717, Size:7807488, MD5 Value:
       EF98DB35796126ABBC04412589FB7932
    08ATA48.003: From:15614976, To:23541205, Size:7807488, MD5 Value:
       C8CFFAC6AB449242BD80E98F1F656FDA
       . . .
    08ATA48.049: From:374759424, To:382685653, Size:7807488, MD5 Value:
       EDE9FDEACC276A2B28900691C92B0DB9
    08ATA48.050: From:382566912, To:390493141, Size:7807488, MD5 Value:
       3175264A9003C5D980DDEB823767DFE6
    08ATA48.051: From:390374400, To:398300629, Size:347568, MD5 Value:
       D881EE19EA1A118FE1A53AD2422AE033
    Settings: error skip
    speed UDMA-5
```

Results:	

Assertion & Expected Result	Actual Result
AM-01 Source acquired using interface AI.	as expected
AM-02 Source is type DS.	as expected
AM-03 Execution environment is XE.	as expected
AM-05 An image is created on file system type FS.	as expected
AM-06 All visible sectors acquired.	as expected
AM-07 All hidden sectors acquired.	as expected
AM-08 All sectors accurately acquired.	as expected
AO-01 Image file is complete and accurate.	as expected
AO-05 Multifile image created.	as expected
AO-22 Tool calculates hashes by block.	as expected
AO-23 Logged information is correct.	as expected
AO-24 Source is unchanged by acquisition.	as expected

Analysis:	Expected results achieved

5.2.17 DA-08-DCO

Test Case DA-08-DCO F-TALON V2.43	
Case Summary:	DA-08 Acquire a physical drive with hidden sectors to an image file.
Assertions:	AM-01 The tool uses access interface SRC-AI to access the digital source. AM-02 The tool acquires digital source DS. AM-03 The tool executes in execution environment XE. AM-05 If image file creation is specified, the tool creates an image file on file system type FS. AM-06 All visible sectors are acquired from the digital source. AM-07 All hidden sectors are acquired from the digital source. AM-08 All sectors acquired from the digital source are acquired accurately. AO-01 If the tool creates an image file, the data represented by the image file is the same as the data acquired by the tool. AO-05 If the tool creates a multi-file image of a requested size then all the individual files shall be no larger than the requested size. AO-22 If requested, the tool calculates block hashes for a specified block size during an acquisition for each block acquired from the digital source. AO-23 If the tool logs any log significant information, the information is accurately recorded in the log file. AO-24 If the tool executes in a forensically safe execution environment, the digital source is unchanged by the acquisition process.
Tester Name:	brl
Test Host:	Athos
Test Date:	Thu Nov 1 14:40:14 2007
Drives:	src(92) dst (none) other (13-IDE)
Source Setup:	src hash (SHA1): < 63E6F7BD3040A8ADA2CF8FBF66A805B76DF10481 > src hash (MD5): < E095DD1BD0B0DD6E603153A3FE1A2F3E > 58633344 total sectors (30020272128 bytes) 58167/015/63 (max cyl/hd values) 58168/016/63 (number of cyl/hd) IDE disk: Model (WDC WD300BB-00CAA0) serial # (WD-WMA8H2140350) N Start LBA Length Start C/H/S End C/H/S boot Partition type 1 P 000000063 058605057 0000/001/01 1023/254/63 Boot 07 NTFS 2 P 000000000 000000000 0000/000/00 0000/000/00 00 empty entry 3 P 000000000 000000000 0000/000/00 0000/000/00 00 empty entry 4 P 000000000 000000000 0000/000/00 0000/000/00 00 empty entry 1 058605057 sectors 30005789184 bytes Hashes with DCO in place: md5:525963C6789423396FE1F3202A8CBD04 sha1.txt:55A3CFE756B7B0034DCCE71F7D7A477D8681B781

Log Highlights:	***** FORENSIC TALON Serial No.: 15881 Software: V2.43 *****
	                  SESSION SETTINGS
	    Operating Mode: DD Img(2GB) Address Mode: LBA
	    Verify : MD5-Disk Speed : UDMA-4
	    Connection : Direct
	         AN EXACT DD IMAGE FILE COPY OF THE SUSPECT DRIVE HAS
	        BEEN SUCCESSFULLY EXECUTED ON THE EVIDENCE DRIVE!
	************************** SOURCE DRIVE **************************
	              Physical Characteristics
	   Drive Model: WDC WD300BB-00CAA0
	     Serial: WD-WMA8H2140350
	     Cylinders Heads Sectors Total Sectors Drive Size
	     58168 16 63 58633344 28.0 GB
	************************ DESTINATION DRIVE **********************
	              Physical Characteristics
	   Drive Model: MAXTOR STM3120814A
	     Serial: 5LS6PD2S
	     Cylinders Heads Sectors Total Sectors Drive Size
	    232581 16 63 234441648 111.8 GB
	    Skipped Sectors: 0 Recovered Sectors: 0
	* Source Drive From:0, To:58633343, Size:58633344, MD5 Value:
	Acquisition Hash
	  Source Drive From:0, To:58633343, Size:58633344, MD5 Value:
	   E095DD1BD0B0DD6E603153A3FE1A2F3E

Test Case DA-08-DCO F-TALON V2.43	
	Settings: error skip speed UDMA-5
Results:	

Assertion & Expected Result	Actual Result
AM-01 Source acquired using interface AI.	as expected
AM-02 Source is type DS.	as expected
AM-03 Execution environment is XE.	as expected
AM-05 An image is created on file system type FS.	as expected
AM-06 All visible sectors acquired.	as expected
AM-07 All hidden sectors acquired.	as expected
AM-08 All sectors accurately acquired.	as expected
AO-01 Image file is complete and accurate.	as expected
AO-05 Multifile image created.	as expected
AO-22 Tool calculates hashes by block.	option not tested
AO-23 Logged information is correct.	as expected
AO-24 Source is unchanged by acquisition.	as expected

Analysis:	Expected results achieved

5.2.18   DA-09-RETRY

Test Case DA-09-RETRY F-TALON V2.43	
Case Summary:	DA-09 Acquire a digital source that has at least one faulty data sector.
Assertions:	AM-01 The tool uses access interface SRC-AI to access the digital source. AM-02 The tool acquires digital source DS. AM-03 The tool executes in execution environment XE. AM-05 If image file creation is specified, the tool creates an image file on file system type FS. AM-06 All visible sectors are acquired from the digital source. AM-08 All sectors acquired from the digital source are acquired accurately. AM-09 If unresolved errors occur while reading from the selected digital source, the tool notifies the user of the error type and location within the digital source. AM-10 If unresolved errors occur while reading from the selected digital source, the tool uses a benign fill in the destination object in place of the inaccessible data. AO-01 If the tool creates an image file, the data represented by the image file is the same as the data acquired by the tool. AO-05 If the tool creates a multi-file image of a requested size then all the individual files shall be no larger than the requested size. AO-22 If requested, the tool calculates block hashes for a specified block size during an acquisition for each block acquired from the digital source. AO-23 If the tool logs any log significant information, the information is accurately recorded in the log file. AO-24 If the tool executes in a forensically safe execution environment, the digital source is unchanged by the acquisition process.
Tester Name:	brl
Test Host:	Athos
Test Date:	Thu Nov 1 15:45:04 2007
Drives:	src(ED-BAD-CPR1) dst (6F) other (none)
Source Setup:	No before hash for ED-BAD-CPR1 120103200 total sectors (61492838400 bytes) Drive with known bad sectors Vendor: Maxtor Model: DiamondMax Plus 9 Known Bad Sector List for ED-CPR-BAD-1 Manufacturer: Maxtor Model: 6Y060L0 DiamondMax Plus 9 Serial Number: Y27KR6CE Capacity: 60GB Interface: PATA 54 faulty sectors 10069095, 10069911, 12023808, 18652594, 18656041, 18656857, 18660303, 18661119, 19746716-19746717, 22233904, 23098370, 23383001, 24102466-24102467, 24104250, 24106656, 24107458, 28959971-28959972, 41825791, 41828995, 52654580, 52655318, 60522984, 68643842-68643843, 69973290, 72714626, 72715293, 82148809, 82148810, 83810525, 85310861, 85313430, 85314038-85314039, 86321211, 86323780, 87186066, 87856313, 87856922, 97191260-97191261, 100093150-100093151, 103861021, 109706975-109706976, 110347947, 110350122-110350123, 115664758, 115835518
Log Highlights:	Destination setup 120103200 sectors wiped with 6F Comparision of original to clone Drive Sectors compared: 120103200 Sectors match: 120103146 Sectors differ: 54 Bytes differ: 27594 Diffs range 10069095, 10069911, 12023808, 18652594, 18656041, 18656857, 18660303, 18661119, 19746716-19746717, 22233904, 23098370, 23383001, 24102466-24102467, 24104250, 24106656, 24107458, 28959971-28959972, 41825791, 41828995,

```
             52654580, 52655318, 60522984, 68643842-68643843, 69973290,
             72714626, 72715293, 82148809-82148810, 83810525, 85310861,
             85313430, 85314038-85314039, 86321211, 86323780, 87186066,
             87856313, 87856922, 97191260-97191261, 100093150-100093151,
             103861021, 109706975-109706976, 110347947, 110350122-110350123,
             115664758, 115835518
             0 source read errors, 0 destination read errors

             *****     FORENSIC TALON     Serial No.: 15881  Software: V2.43     *****
                                SESSION SETTINGS
                Operating Mode: Capture           Address Mode: LBA
                Verify      : None                  Speed   : PIO-AUTO
                Connection  : Direct
                          100% MIRROR COPY OF THE SUSPECT DRIVE HAS BEEN
                          SUCCESSFULLY EXECUTED ON THE EVIDENCE DRIVE!
                          No Destination Drive erase required!
             *************************   SOURCE DRIVE   *************************
                                Physical Characteristics
                Drive Model: Maxtor 6Y060L0
                     Serial: Y27KR6CE
                   Cylinders   Heads    Sectors    Total Sectors    Drive Size
                    119150       16        63         120103200       57.3 GB
                     Computed SHA-256 Value:  NONE
                Recovered Sectors: 0        Unrecovered/Skipped Sectors: 54
             *********************   DESTINATION DRIVE   *********************
                                Physical Characteristics
                Drive Model: Maxtor 6Y060L0
                     Serial: Y2VVJJ5E
                   Cylinders   Heads    Sectors    Total Sectors    Drive Size
                    119150       16        63         120103200       57.3 GB
                     Computed SHA-256 Value:  NONE
                        Skipped Sector Addresses:
                   10069095   10069911   12023808   18652594   18656041   18656857
                   18660303   18661119   19746716   19746717   22233904   23098370
                   23383001   24102466   24102467   24104250   24106656   24107458
                   28959971   28959972   41825791   41828995   52654580   52655318
                   60522984   68643842   68643843   69973290   72714626   72715293
                   82148809   82148810   83810525   85310861   85313430   85314038
                   85314039   86321211   86323780   87186066   87856313   87856922
                   97191260   97191261   100093150  100093151  103861021  109706975
                   109706976  110347947  110350122  110350123  115664758  115835518
                        Skipped Sectors: 54    Recovered Sectors: 0
                Recovered Sectors: 0           Unrecovered/Skipped Sectors: 54
                        Skipped Sector Addresses:
                        Skipped Sectors: 54    Recovered Sectors: 0
             2 different run lengths observed in 44 runs
             34 runs of length 1
             10 runs of length 2
             54 sectors differ
                54 zero filled and 0 varying non-zero filled
             Settings: error retry
             speed PIO-AUTO
```

Results:

Assertion & Expected Result	Actual Result
AM-01 Source acquired using interface AI.	as expected
AM-02 Source is type DS.	as expected
AM-03 Execution environment is XE.	as expected
AM-05 An image is created on file system type FS.	as expected
AM-06 All visible sectors acquired.	as expected
AM-08 All sectors accurately acquired.	as expected
AM-09 Error logged.	as expected
AM-10 Benign fill replaces inaccessible sectors.	as expected
AO-01 Image file is complete and accurate.	as expected
AO-05 Multifile image created.	as expected
AO-22 Tool calculates hashes by block.	option not tested
AO-23 Logged information is correct.	as expected
AO-24 Source is unchanged by acquisition.	not checked

Test Case DA-09-RETRY F-TALON V2.43	
Analysis:	Expected results achieved

5.2.19　DA-09-RETRY-SATA

Test Case DA-09-RETRY-SATA F-TALON V2.43	
Case Summary:	DA-09 Acquire a digital source that has at least one faulty data sector.
Assertions:	AM-01 The tool uses access interface SRC-AI to access the digital source. AM-02 The tool acquires digital source DS. AM-03 The tool executes in execution environment XE. AM-05 If image file creation is specified, the tool creates an image file on file system type FS. AM-06 All visible sectors are acquired from the digital source. AM-08 All sectors acquired from the digital source are acquired accurately. AM-09 If unresolved errors occur while reading from the selected digital source, the tool notifies the user of the error type and location within the digital source. AM-10 If unresolved errors occur while reading from the selected digital source, the tool uses a benign fill in the destination object in place of the inaccessible data. AO-01 If the tool creates an image file, the data represented by the image file is the same as the data acquired by the tool. AO-05 If the tool creates a multi-file image of a requested size then all the individual files shall be no larger than the requested size. AO-22 If requested, the tool calculates block hashes for a specified block size during an acquisition for each block acquired from the digital source. AO-23 If the tool logs any log significant information, the information is accurately recorded in the log file. AO-24 If the tool executes in a forensically safe execution environment, the digital source is unchanged by the acquisition process.
Tester Name:	brl
Test Host:	Max
Test Date:	Tue Nov 6 15:14:35 2007
Drives:	src(ED-BAD-CPR2) dst (22-SATA) other (none)
Source Setup:	No before hash for ED-BAD-CPR2 Known Bad Sector List for ED-CPR-BAD-2 Manufacturer: Maxtor Model: DiamondMax Plus 9 Serial Number: Y22HJL7C Capacity: 60GB Interface: SATA 468 faulty sectors 1344585, 2594747, 2595500, 2599086, 2599839, 2809909, 2809910, 3422895, 3422896, 4116750, 4120336, 4120337, 4121089, 4121090, 4696046, 4698397, 4703710, 4707186, 4708105, 4711580, 4712499, 4714850, 4715770, 4719245, 4723639, 4723640, 4724558, 4724559, 4728034, 4728953, 4731304, 4732223, 4735699, 4740093, 4741012, 4743363, 4745407, 4748677, 4752152, 4756547, 4757466, 4759817, 4761860, 4761861, 4764211, 4764212, 4765130, 4765131, 4768606, 4769525, 4773001, 4773920, 4776271, 4777190, 4780665, 4781584, 5446946, 5448990, 5451341, 5452260, 5620120, 5623595, 5623596, 5623597, 5624514, 5624515, 5624516, 5626865, 5626866, 5626867, 5628909, 5631260, 5632179, 5635655, 5636574, 5640049, 6021518, 6023869, 6024788, 6028263, 7662307, 8340091, 8340092, 12178157, 12179060, 12181370, 12182273, 12185687, 12186590, 12340277, 13016906, 13049575, 13050477, 13050478, 14000022, 14000762, 14004285, 14041240, 17135988, 17723611, 17876726, 18161032, 18760155, 20090856, 20094289, 20095011, 20661414, 21693295, 21694174, 21697502, 22730717, 22838734, 22838735, 24596104, 24596105, 24596106, 26791779, 27686030, 28080041, 28081995, 29555383, 29655054, 30488210, 30488211, 32215323, 32218669, 33523139, 33991449, 35267814, 37975363, 38134596, 38136734, 38137571, 38137572, 38207258, 38207259, 38542983, 38567425, 38568109, 39421072, 39421909, 39425071, 40273501, 42836488, 42837172, 42843548, 42847497, 42851446, 42854557, 43505180,

```
              43508342, 43872574, 43873411, 45217120, 45217121, 45777316,
              46221189, 46296219, 46296220, 46528674, 46955925, 47093653,
              48537000, 48537662, 49911188, 49911189, 51017721, 51769307,
              51769969, 51994516, 51994517, 53855354, 55793018, 55793019,
              57316559, 57320313, 60571670, 60571671, 60571672, 60952349,
              60952350, 60952993, 61535962, 61535963, 61535964, 62592910,
              62593672, 62596563, 62597325, 62600215, 63140751, 63140752,
              63141513, 63141514, 63144404, 63226363, 63229253, 63670246,
              63972517, 63975497, 65576815, 65925948, 66146215, 67860503,
              67860504, 68711104, 69100751, 69176705, 69189596, 69189597,
              69189598, 69190358, 69190359, 69190360, 69974439, 69975201,
              70656792, 72217315, 72801392, 72992581, 72992582, 73626901,
              73626902, 75004819, 78164515, 78167178, 78167885, 78307369,
              78415033, 78415034, 78693137, 79145838, 79146544, 79146545,
              79146546, 79744714, 79745420, 79748084, 79748790, 79901007,
              80691204, 80691205, 82083870, 82083871, 82083872, 83739051,
              83739052, 84411502, 84553520, 85181194, 85418740, 87197252,
              88020545, 88020546, 88021216, 88023752, 88024422, 88071013,
              88071014, 88755730, 89294003, 92741348, 92741349, 92743744,
              92743745, 94017998, 95929572, 95929573, 97369221, 97485310,
              99685572, 100687317, 100689593, 102205339, 103403045,
              104768238, 105074641, 105638643, 106115226, 106115791,
              106117947, 106118512, 106120668, 106121233, 106122698,
              106123954, 106123955, 106125419, 106125420, 106125984,
              106125985, 106128141, 106128706, 106186051, 106936608,
              107133037, 107276378, 108007258, 109270108, 109270673,
              109272829, 109273394, 109275550, 109319902, 110072175,
              111250371, 111251549, 111485059, 112587333, 112588682,
              112588683, 112588684, 114286586, 114359887, 115110935,
              116807008, 116807009, 116808918, 117175664, 117177512,
              117178002, 117179850, 117180340, 117180341, 117181588,
              117182678, 117182679, 117182680, 117183929, 117184417,
              117186264, 117186265, 117186755, 117188602, 117188603,
              117188604, 117189093, 117190341, 117193170, 117195017,
              117195018, 117195508, 117197355, 117197356, 117197357,
              117197846, 117199094, 117199584, 117201432, 117201922,
              117201923, 117203770, 117204260, 117204261, 117204262,
              117205508, 117206599, 117207846, 117207847, 117207848,
              117208337, 117210185, 117210675, 117212523, 117213013,
              117213014, 117214261, 117215352, 117217090, 117218938,
              117219428, 117219429, 117221276, 117221766, 117221767,
              117221768, 117223014, 117223505, 117225352, 117225353,
              117225354, 117225843, 117227691, 117228181, 117229429,
              117230519, 117230520, 117231767, 117232258, 117234105,
              117234106, 117234596, 117236934, 117238182,
              117239272, 117239273, 117240520, 117241011, 117242858,
              117242859, 117245687, 117245688, 117246935, 117247426,
              117249273, 117249274, 117249764, 117251612, 117252102,
              117253350, 117254440, 117254441, 117255688, 117256179,
              117258026, 117258027, 117258517, 117260365, 117260855,
              117262103, 117263193, 117263194, 117264441, 117264932,
              117266779, 117266118, 117267270, 117269118, 117269608,
              117270856, 117271946, 117271947, 117275533, 117276023,
              117277871, 117278361, 117278362, 117278363, 117279609,
              117280100, 117281947, 117281948, 117282438, 117284286,
              117284776, 117286024, 117287114, 117287115, 117287116,
              117288362, 117288853, 117290700, 117290701, 117290702,
              117291191, 117293039, 117293529, 117294777, 117295867,
              117295868, 117295869, 117297115, 117297606, 117299453,
              117299454, 117299455, 119655644
```

Log Highlights:	Destination setup
	156301488 sectors wiped with 22
	Comparision of original to clone Drive
	Sectors compared: 120103200
	Sectors match: 120102732
	Sectors differ: 468
	Bytes differ: 239148
	Diffs range 1344585, 2594747, 2595500, 2599086, 2599839,

```
2809909-2809910, 3422895-3422896, 4116750, 4120336-4120337,
4121089-4121090, 4696046, 4698397, 4703710, 4707186,
4708105, 4711580, 4712499, 4714850, 4715770, 4719245,
4723639-4723640, 4724558-4724559, 4728034, 4728953,
4731304, 4732223, 4735699, 4740093, 4741012, 4743363,
4745407, 4748677, 4752152, 4756547, 4757466, 4759817,
4761860-4761861, 4764211-4764212, 4765130-4765131,
4768606, 4769525, 4773001, 4773920, 4776271, 4777190,
4780665, 4781584, 5446946, 5448990, 5451341, 5452260,
5620120, 5623595-5623597, 5624514-5624516, 5626865-5626867,
5628909, 5631260, 5632179, 5635655, 5636574, 5640049,
6021518, 6023869, 6024788, 6028263, 7662307, 8340091-8340092,
12178157, 12179060, 12181370, 12182273, 12185687, 12186590,
12340277, 13016906, 13049575, 13050477-13050478, 14000022,
14000762, 14004285, 14041240, 17135988, 17723611, 17876726,
18161032, 18760155, 20090856, 20094289, 20095011, 20661414,
21693295, 21694174, 21697502, 22730717, 22838734-22838735,
24596104-24596106, 26791779, 27686030, 28080041, 28081995,
29555383, 29655054, 30488210-30488211, 32215323, 32218669,
33523139, 33991449, 35267814, 37975363, 38134596, 38136734,
38137571-38137572, 38207258-38207259, 38542983, 38567425,
38568109, 39421072, 39421909, 39425071, 40273501, 42836488,
42837172, 42843548, 42847497, 42851446, 42854557, 43505180,
43508342, 43872574, 43873411, 45217120-45217121, 45777316,
46221189, 46296219-46296220, 46528674, 46955925, 47093653,
48537000, 48537662, 49911188-49911189, 51017721, 51769307,
51769969, 51994516-51994517, 53855354, 55793018-55793019,
57316559, 57320313, 60571670-60571672, 60952349-60952350,
60952993, 61535962-61535964, 62592910, 62593672, 62596563,
62597325, 62600215, 63140751-63140752, 63141513-63141514,
63144404, 63226363, 63229253, 63670246, 63972517, 63975497,
65576815, 65925948, 66146215, 67860503-67860504, 68711104,
69100751, 69176705, 69189596-69189598, 69190358-69190360,
69974439, 69975201, 70656792, 72217315, 72801392, 72992581-72992582,
73626901-73626902, 75004819, 78164515, 78167178, 78167885,
78307369, 78415033-78415034, 78693137, 79145838, 79146544-79146546,
79744714, 79745420, 79748084, 79748790, 79901007, 80691204-80691205,
82083870-82083872, 83739051-83739052, 84411502, 84553520,
85181194, 85418740, 87197252, 88020545-88020546, 88021216,
88023752, 88024422, 88071013-88071014, 88755730, 89294003,
92741348-92741349, 92743744-92743745, 94017998, 95929572-95929573,
97369221, 97485310, 99685572, 100687317, 100689593,
102205779, 102403045, 104768238, 105074641, 105638643,
106115226, 106115791, 106117947, 106118512, 106120668,
106121233, 106122698, 106123954-106123955, 106125419-106125420,
106125984-106125985, 106128141, 106128706, 106186051,
106936608, 107133037, 107276378, 108007258, 109270108,
109270673, 109272829, 109273394, 109275550, 109319902,
110072175, 111250371, 111251549, 111485059, 112587333,
112588682-112588684, 114286586, 114359887, 115110935,
116807008-116807009, 116808918, 117175664, 117177512,
117178002, 117179850, 117180340-117180341, 117181588,
117182678-117182680, 117183926, 117184417, 117186264-117186265,
117186755, 117188602-117188604, 117189093, 117190341,
117193170, 117195017-117195018, 117195508, 117197355-117197357,
117197846, 117199094, 117199584, 117201432, 117201922-117201923,
117203770, 117204260-117204262, 117205508, 117206599,
117207846-117207848, 117208337, 117210185, 117210675,
117212523, 117213013-117213014, 117214261, 117215352,
117217090, 117218938, 117219428-117219429, 117221276,
117221766-117221768, 117223014, 117223505, 117225352-117225354,
117225843, 117227691, 117228181, 117229429, 117230519-117230520,
117231767, 117232258, 117234105-117234106, 117234596,
117236444, 117236934, 117238182, 117239272-117239273,
117240520, 117241011, 117242858-117242859, 117245687-117245688,
117246935, 117247426, 117249273-117249274, 117249764,
117251612, 117252102, 117253350, 117254440-117254441,
117255688, 117256179, 117258026-117258027, 117258517,
117260365, 117260855, 117262103, 117263193-117263194,
117264441, 117264932, 117266779-117266780, 117267270,
```

```
117269118, 117269608, 117270856, 117271946-117271947,
117275533, 117276023, 117277871, 117278361-117278363,
117279609, 117280100, 117281947-117281948, 117282438,
117284286, 117284776, 117286024, 117287114-117287116,
117288362, 117288853, 117290700-117290702, 117291191,
117293039, 117293529, 117294777, 117295867-117295869,
117297115, 117297606, 117299453-117299455, 119655644
Source (120103200) has 36198288 fewer sectors than destination (156301488)
Zero fill:            0
Src Byte fill (ED):   0
Dst Byte fill (22): 36198288
Other fill:          0
Other no fill:       0
Zero fill range:
Src fill range:
Dst fill range:  120103200-156301487
Other fill range:
Other not filled range:
0 source read errors, 0 destination read errors

*****     FORENSIC TALON     Serial No.: 15881  Software: V2.43    *****
                       SESSION SETTINGS
     Operating Mode: Capture        Address Mode: LBA
     Verify     : HW-MD5            Speed   : PIO-AUTO
     Connection : Direct
              100% MIRROR COPY OF THE SUSPECT DRIVE HAS BEEN
               SUCCESSFULLY EXECUTED ON THE EVIDENCE DRIVE!
        Operator declined FULL and remainder Destination Drive erase!
************************   SOURCE DRIVE   ************************
                     Physical Characteristics
    Drive Model: Maxtor 6Y060M0
         Serial: Y22HJL7C
       Cylinders   Heads    Sectors     Total Sectors     Drive Size
        119150       16        63         120103200         57.3 GB
         Computed MD5 Value: E288054C AA3E56B1 218FBD8E A2EEB940
    Recovered Sectors: 0        Unrecovered/Skipped Sectors: 468
**********************   DESTINATION DRIVE   **********************
                     Physical Characteristics
    Drive Model: ST380013AS
         Serial: 5JVCQ731
       Cylinders   Heads    Sectors     Total Sectors     Drive Size
        155061       16        63         156301488         74.5 GB
         Computed SHA-256 Value:  NONE
        Skipped Sector Addresses:
     1344585    2594747    2595500    2599086    2599839    2809909
     2809910    3422895    3422896    4116750    4120336    4120337
     4121089    4121090    4696046    4698397    4703710    4707186
     4708105    4711580    4712499    4714850    4715770    4719245
     4723639    4723640    4724558    4724559    4728034    4728953
     4731304    4732223    4735699    4740093    4741012    4743363
     4745407    4748677    4752152    4756547    4757466    4759817
     4761860    4761861    4764211    4764212    4765130    4765131
     4768606    4769525    4773001    4773920    4776271    4777190
     4780665    4781584    5446946    5448990    5451341    5452260
     5620120    5623595    5623596    5623597    5624514    5624515
     5624516    5626865    5626866    5626867    5628909    5631260
     5632179    5635655    5636574    5640049    6021518    6023869
     6024788    6028263    7662307    8340091    8340092   12178157
    12179060   12181370   12182273   12185687   12186590   12340277
    13016906   13049575   13050477   13050478   14000022   14000762
    14004285   14041240   17135988   17723611   17876726   18161032
    18760155   20090856   20094289   20095011   20661414   21693295
    21694174   21697502   22730717   22838734   22838735   24596104
    24596105   24596106   26791779   27686030   28080041   28081995
    29555383   29655054   30488210   30488211   32215323   32218669
    33523139   33991449   35267814   37975843   38134596   38136734
    38137571   38137572   38207258   38207259   38542983   38567425
    38568109   39421072   39421909   39425071   40273501   42836488
    42837172   42843548   42847497   42851446   42854557   43505180
    43508342   43872574   43873411   45217120   45217121   45777316
```

```
          46221189    46296219    46296220    46528674    46955925    47093653
          48537000    48537662    49911188    49911189    51017721    51769307
          51769969    51994516    51994517    53855354    55793018    55793019
          57316559    57320313    60571670    60571671    60571672    60952349
          60952350    60952993    61535962    61535963    61535964    62592910
          62593672    62596563    62597325    62600215    63140751    63140752
          63141513    63141514    63144404    63226363    63229253    63670246
          63972517    63975497
              Skipped Sectors: 468    Recovered Sectors: 0
          Recovered Sectors: 0          Unrecovered/Skipped Sectors: 468
              Skipped Sector Addresses:
              Skipped Sectors: 468    Recovered Sectors: 0
    3 different run lengths observed in 366 runs
    287 runs of length 1
    56 runs of length 2
    23 runs of length 3
    468 sectors differ
        468 zero filled and 0 varying non-zero filled
    Settings: error retry
    speed PIO-AUTO
```

Results:	

Assertion & Expected Result	Actual Result
AM-01 Source acquired using interface AI.	as expected
AM-02 Source is type DS.	as expected
AM-03 Execution environment is XE.	as expected
AM-05 An image is created on file system type FS.	as expected
AM-06 All visible sectors acquired.	as expected
AM-08 All sectors accurately acquired.	as expected
AM-09 Error logged.	as expected
AM-10 Benign fill replaces inaccessible sectors.	as expected
AO-01 Image file is complete and accurate.	as expected
AO-05 Multifile image created.	as expected
AO-22 Tool calculates hashes by block.	option not tested
AO-23 Logged information is correct.	as expected
AO-24 Source is unchanged by acquisition.	not checked

Analysis:	Expected results achieved

5.2.20   DA-09-SKIP-ATA

Test Case DA-09-SKIP-ATA F-TALON V2.43	
Case Summary:	DA-09 Acquire a digital source that has at least one faulty data sector.
Assertions:	AM-01 The tool uses access interface SRC-AI to access the digital source. AM-02 The tool acquires digital source DS. AM-03 The tool executes in execution environment XE. AM-05 If image file creation is specified, the tool creates an image file on file system type FS. AM-06 All visible sectors are acquired from the digital source. AM-08 All sectors acquired from the digital source are acquired accurately. AM-09 If unresolved errors occur while reading from the selected digital source, the tool notifies the user of the error type and location within the digital source. AM-10 If unresolved errors occur while reading from the selected digital source, the tool uses a benign fill in the destination object in place of the inaccessible data. AO-01 If the tool creates an image file, the data represented by the image file is the same as the data acquired by the tool. AO-05 If the tool creates a multi-file image of a requested size then all the individual files shall be no larger than the requested size. AO-22 If requested, the tool calculates block hashes for a specified block size during an acquisition for each block acquired from the digital source. AO-23 If the tool logs any log significant information, the information is accurately recorded in the log file. AO-24 If the tool executes in a forensically safe execution environment, the digital source is unchanged by the acquisition process.
Tester Name:	brl
Test Host:	SamSpade
Test Date:	Wed Nov 14 10:59:09 2007
Drives:	src(ED-BAD-CPR1) dst (80) other (none)

Source Setup:	No before hash for ED-BAD-CPR1
	  120103200 total sectors (61492838400 bytes)
	  Drive with known bad sectors
	  Vendor: Maxtor Model: DiamondMax Plus 9
	
	Known Bad Sector List for ED-CPR-BAD-1
	
	Manufacturer: Maxtor
	Model: 6Y060L0 DiamondMax Plus 9
	Serial Number: Y27KR6CE
	Capacity: 60GB
	Interface: PATA
	
	54 faulty sectors
	10069095, 10069911, 12023808, 18652594, 18656041, 18656857, 18660303, 18661119, 19746716-19746717, 22233904, 23098370, 23383001, 24102466-24102467, 24104250, 24106656, 24107458, 28959971-28959972, 41825791, 41828995, 52654580, 52655318, 60522984, 68643842-68643843, 69973290, 72714626, 72715293, 82148809, 82148810, 83810525, 85310861, 85313430, 85314038-85314039, 86321211, 86323780, 87186066, 87856313, 87856922, 97191260-97191261, 100093150-100093151, 103861021, 109706975-109706976, 110347947, 110350122-110350123, 115664758, 115835518

Log Highlights:	Destination setup 156301488 sectors wiped with 80 Comparision of original to clone Drive Sectors compared: 120103200 Sectors match: 120103146 Sectors differ: 54 Bytes differ: 27594 Diffs range 10069095, 10069911, 12023808, 18652594, 18656041, 18656857, 18660303, 18661119, 19746716-19746717, 22233904, 23098370, 23383001, 24102466-24102467, 24104250, 24106656, 24107458, 28959971-28959972, 41825791, 41828995,

```
52654580, 52655318, 60522984, 68643842-68643843, 69973290,
72714626, 72715293, 82148809-82148810, 83810525, 85310861,
85313430, 85314038-85314039, 86321211, 86323780, 87186066,
87856313, 87856922, 97191260-97191261, 100093150-100093151,
103861021, 109706975-109706976, 110347947, 110350122-110350123,
115664758, 115835518
Source (120103200) has 36198288 fewer sectors than destination (156301488)
Zero fill:                 0
Src Byte fill (ED):        0
Dst Byte fill (80): 36198288
Other fill:                0
Other no fill:             0
Zero fill range:
Src fill range:
Dst fill range:  120103200-156301487
Other fill range:
Other not filled range:
0 source read errors, 0 destination read errors

*****      FORENSIC TALON     Serial No.: 15881  Software: V2.43     *****
                          SESSION SETTINGS
        Operating Mode: Capture          Address Mode: LBA
        Verify      : None          Speed    : PIO-AUTO
        Connection  : Direct
                 100% MIRROR COPY OF THE SUSPECT DRIVE HAS BEEN
                 SUCCESSFULLY EXECUTED ON THE EVIDENCE DRIVE!
        Operator declined FULL and remainder Destination Drive erase!
     ************************      SOURCE DRIVE      ************************
                      Physical Characteristics
     Drive Model: Maxtor 6Y060L0
         Serial: Y27KR6CE
        Cylinders    Heads    Sectors    Total Sectors    Drive Size
         119150       16        63          120103200       57.3 GB
            Computed SHA-256 Value:  NONE
                        Skipped Sectors: 54
     ************************   DESTINATION DRIVE   ************************
                      Physical Characteristics
     Drive Model: WDC WD800BB-00CAA1
         Serial: WD-WCA8E5174999
        Cylinders    Heads    Sectors    Total Sectors    Drive Size
         155061       16        63          156301488       74.5 GB
            Computed SHA-256 Value:  NONE
              Skipped Sector Addresses:
        10069095   10069911   12023808   18652594   18656041   18656857
        18660303   18661119   19746716   19746717   22233904   23098370
        23383001   24102466   24102467   24104250   24106656   24107458
        28959971   28959972   41825791   41828995   52654580   52655318
        60522984   68643842   68643843   69973290   72714626   72715293
        82148809   82148810   83810525   85310861   85313430   85314038
        85314039   86321211   86323780   87186066   87856313   87856922
        97191260   97191261   100093150  100093151  103861021  109706975
        109706976  110347947  110350122  110350123  115664758  115835518
           Skipped Sectors: 54    Recovered Sectors: 0
                      Skipped Sectors: 54
           Skipped Sector Addresses:
           Skipped Sectors: 54    Recovered Sectors: 0
2 different run lengths observed in 44 runs
34 runs of length 1
10 runs of length 2
54 sectors differ
   54 zero filled and 0 varying non-zero filled
Settings: error skip
speed PIO-AUTO
```

	Assertion & Expected Result	Actual Result
Results:	AM-01 Source acquired using interface AI.	as expected
	AM-02 Source is type DS.	as expected
	AM-03 Execution environment is XE.	as expected

Test Case DA-09-SKIP-ATA F-TALON V2.43		
	AM-05 An image is created on file system type FS.	as expected
	AM-06 All visible sectors acquired.	as expected
	AM-08 All sectors accurately acquired.	as expected
	AM-09 Error logged.	as expected
	AM-10 Benign fill replaces inaccessible sectors.	as expected
	AO-01 Image file is complete and accurate.	as expected
	AO-05 Multifile image created.	as expected
	AO-22 Tool calculates hashes by block.	option not tested
	AO-23 Logged information is correct.	as expected
	AO-24 Source is unchanged by acquisition.	not checked
Analysis:	Expected results achieved	

5.2.21 DA-09-SKIP-SATA

Test Case DA-09-SKIP-SATA F-TALON V2.43	
Case Summary:	DA-09 Acquire a digital source that has at least one faulty data sector.
Assertions:	AM-01 The tool uses access interface SRC-AI to access the digital source. AM-02 The tool acquires digital source DS. AM-03 The tool executes in execution environment XE. AM-05 If image file creation is specified, the tool creates an image file on file system type FS. AM-06 All visible sectors are acquired from the digital source. AM-08 All sectors acquired from the digital source are acquired accurately. AM-09 If unresolved errors occur while reading from the selected digital source, the tool notifies the user of the error type and location within the digital source. AM-10 If unresolved errors occur while reading from the selected digital source, the tool uses a benign fill in the destination object in place of the inaccessible data. AO-01 If the tool creates an image file, the data represented by the image file is the same as the data acquired by the tool. AO-05 If the tool creates a multi-file image of a requested size then all the individual files shall be no larger than the requested size. AO-22 If requested, the tool calculates block hashes for a specified block size during an acquisition for each block acquired from the digital source. AO-23 If the tool logs any log significant information, the information is accurately recorded in the log file. AO-24 If the tool executes in a forensically safe execution environment, the digital source is unchanged by the acquisition process.
Tester Name:	brl
Test Host:	Athos
Test Date:	Wed Nov 7 11:27:28 2007
Drives:	src(ED-BAD-CPR2) dst (23-SATA) other (none)
Source Setup:	No before hash for ED-BAD-CPR2 Known Bad Sector List for ED-CPR-BAD-2 Manufacturer: Maxtor Model: DiamondMax Plus 9 Serial Number: Y22HJL7C Capacity: 60GB Interface: SATA 468 faulty sectors 1344585, 2594747, 2595500, 2599086, 2599839, 2809909, 2809910, 3422895, 3422896, 4116750, 4120336, 4120337, 4121089, 4121090, 4696046, 4698397, 4703710, 4707186, 4708105, 4711580, 4712499, 4714850, 4715770, 4719245, 4723639, 4723640, 4724558, 4724559, 4728034, 4728953, 4731304, 4732223, 4735699, 4740093, 4741012, 4743363, 4745407, 4748677, 4752152, 4756547, 4757466, 4759817, 4761860, 4761861, 4764211, 4764212, 4765130, 4765131, 4768606, 4769525, 4773001, 4773920, 4776271, 4777190, 4780665, 4781584, 5446946, 5448990, 5451341, 5452260, 5620120, 5623595, 5623596, 5623597, 5624514, 5624515, 5624516, 5626865, 5626866, 5626867, 5628909, 5631260, 5632179, 5635655, 5636574, 5640049, 6021518, 6023869, 6024788, 6028263, 7662307, 8340091, 8340092, 12178157, 12179060, 12181370, 12182273, 12185687, 12186590, 12340277, 13016906, 13049575, 13050477, 13050478, 14000022, 14000762, 14004285, 14041240, 17135988, 17723611, 17876726, 18161032, 18760155, 20090856, 20094289, 20095011, 20661414, 21693295, 21694174, 21697502, 22730717, 22838734, 22838735, 24596104, 24596105, 24596106, 26791779, 27686030, 28080041, 28081995, 29555383, 29655054, 30488210, 30488211, 32215323, 32218669, 33523139, 33991449, 35267814, 37975363, 38134596, 38136734, 38137571, 38137572, 38207258, 38207259, 38542983, 38567425, 38568109, 39421072, 39421909, 39425071, 40273501, 42836488, 42837172, 42843548, 42847497, 42851446, 42854557, 43505180,

August 2009Logicube Forensic Talon 12 14 2009.doc   55 of 62   **Test Resul**

```
                 43508342, 43872574, 43873411, 45217120, 45217121, 45777316,
                 46221189, 46296219, 46296220, 46528674, 46955925, 47093653,
                 48537000, 48537662, 49911188, 49911189, 51017721, 51769307,
                 51769969, 51994516, 51994517, 53855354, 55793018, 55793019,
                 57316559, 57320313, 60571670, 60571671, 60571672, 60952349,
                 60952350, 60952993, 61535962, 61535963, 61535964, 62592910,
                 62593672, 62596563, 62597325, 62600215, 63140751, 63140752,
                 63141513, 63141514, 63144404, 63226363, 63229253, 63670246,
                 63972517, 63975497, 65576815, 65925948, 66146215, 67860503,
                 67860504, 68711104, 69100751, 69176705, 69189596, 69189597,
                 69189598, 69190358, 69190359, 69190360, 69974439, 69975201,
                 70656792, 72217315, 72801392, 72992581, 72992582, 73626901,
                 73626902, 75004819, 78164515, 78167178, 78167885, 78307369,
                 78415033, 78415034, 78693137, 79145838, 79146544, 79146545,
                 79146546, 79744714, 79745420, 79748084, 79748790, 79901007,
                 80691204, 80691205, 82083870, 82083871, 82083872, 83739051,
                 83739052, 84411502, 84553520, 85181194, 85418740, 87197252,
                 88020545, 88020546, 88021216, 88023752, 88024422, 88071013,
                 88071014, 88755730, 89294003, 92741348, 92741349, 92743744,
                 92743745, 94017998, 95929572, 95929573, 97369221, 97485310,
                 99685572, 100687317, 100689593, 102205339, 103403045,
                 104768238, 105074641, 105638643, 106115226, 106115791,
                 106117947, 106118512, 106120668, 106121233, 106122698,
                 106123954, 106123955, 106125419, 106125420, 106125984,
                 106125985, 106128141, 106128706, 106186051, 106936608,
                 107133037, 107276378, 108007258, 109270108, 109270673,
                 109272829, 109273394, 109275550, 109319902, 110072175,
                 111250371, 111251549, 111485059, 112587333, 112588682,
                 112588683, 112588684, 114286586, 114359887, 115110935,
                 116807008, 116807009, 116808918, 117175664, 117177512,
                 117178002, 117179850, 117180340, 117180341, 117181588,
                 117182678, 117182679, 117182680, 117183926, 117184417,
                 117186264, 117186265, 117186755, 117188602, 117188603,
                 117188604, 117189093, 117190341, 117193170, 117195017,
                 117195018, 117195508, 117197355, 117197356, 117197357,
                 117197846, 117199094, 117199584, 117201432, 117201922,
                 117201923, 117203770, 117204260, 117204261, 117204262,
                 117205508, 117206599, 117207846, 117207847, 117207848,
                 117208337, 117210185, 117210675, 117212523, 117213013,
                 117213014, 117214261, 117215352, 117217090, 117218938,
                 117219428, 117219429, 117221276, 117221766, 117221767,
                 117221768, 117223014, 117223505, 117225352, 117225353,
                 117225354, 117225843, 117227691, 117228181, 117229429,
                 117230519, 117230520, 117231767, 117232258, 117234105,
                 117234106, 117234594, 117236444, 117236934, 117238182,
                 117239272, 117239273, 117240520, 117241011, 117242858,
                 117242859, 117245687, 117245688, 117246935, 117247426,
                 117249273, 117249274, 117249764, 117251612, 117252102,
                 117253350, 117254440, 117254441, 117255688, 117256179,
                 117258026, 117258027, 117258517, 117260365, 117260855,
                 117262103, 117263193, 117263194, 117264441, 117264932,
                 117266779, 117266780, 117269270, 117269607, 117269608,
                 117270856, 117271946, 117271947, 117275533, 117276023,
                 117277871, 117278361, 117278362, 117278363, 117279609,
                 117280100, 117281947, 117281948, 117282438, 117284286,
                 117284776, 117286024, 117287114, 117287115, 117287116,
                 117288362, 117288853, 117290700, 117290701, 117290702,
                 117291191, 117293039, 117293529, 117294777, 117295867,
                 117295868, 117295869, 117297115, 117297606, 117299453,
                 117299454, 117299455, 119655644
```

Log Highlights:	Destination setup 156301488 sectors wiped with 23 Comparision of original to clone Drive Sectors compared: 120103200 Sectors match: 120102732 Sectors differ: 468 Bytes differ: 239148 Diffs range 1344585, 2594747, 2595500, 2599086, 2599839,

2809909-2809910, 3422895-3422896, 4116750, 4120336-4120337,
4121089-4121090, 4696046, 4698397, 4703710, 4707186,
4708105, 4711580, 4712499, 4714850, 4715770, 4719245,
4723639-4723640, 4724558-4724559, 4728034, 4728953,
4731304, 4732223, 4735699, 4740093, 4741012, 4743363,
4745407, 4748677, 4752152, 4756547, 4757466, 4759817,
4761860-4761861, 4764211-4764212, 4765130-4765131,
4768606, 4769525, 4773001, 4773920, 4776271, 4777190,
4780665, 4781584, 5446946, 5448990, 5451341, 5452260,
5620120, 5623595-5623597, 5624514-5624516, 5626865-5626867,
5628909, 5631260, 5632179, 5635655, 5636574, 5640049,
6021518, 6023869, 6024788, 6028263, 7662307, 8340091-8340092,
12178157, 12179060, 12181370, 12182273, 12185687, 12186590,
12340277, 13016906, 13049575, 13050477-13050478, 14000022,
14000762, 14004285, 14041240, 17135988, 17723611, 17876726,
18161032, 18760155, 20090856, 20094289, 20095011, 20661414,
21693295, 21694174, 21697502, 22730717, 22838734-22838735,
24596104-24596106, 26791779, 27686030, 28080041, 28081995,
29555383, 29655054, 30488210-30488211, 32215323, 32218669,
33523139, 33991449, 35267814, 37975363, 38134596, 38136734,
38137571-38137572, 38207258-38207259, 38542983, 38567425,
38568109, 39421072, 39421909, 39425071, 40273501, 42836488,
42837172, 42843548, 42847497, 42851446, 42854557, 43505180,
43508342, 43872574, 43873411, 45217120-45217121, 45777316,
46221189, 46296219-46296220, 46528674, 46955925, 47093653,
48537000, 48537662, 49911188-49911189, 51017721, 51769307,
51769969, 51994516-51994517, 53855354, 55793018-55793019,
57316559, 57320313, 60571670-60571672, 60952349-60952350,
60952993, 61535962-61535964, 62592910, 62593672, 62596563,
62597325, 62600215, 63140751-63140752, 63141513-63141514,
63144404, 63226363, 63229253, 63670246, 63972517, 63975497,
65576815, 65925948, 66146215, 67860503-67860504, 68711104,
69100751, 69176705, 69189596-69189598, 69190358-69190360,
69974439, 69975201, 70656792, 72217315, 72801392, 72992581-72992582,
73626901-73626902, 75004819, 78164515, 78167178, 78167885,
78307369, 78415033-78415034, 78693137, 79145838, 79146544-79146546,
79744714, 79745420, 79748084, 79748790, 79901007, 80691204-80691205,
82083870-82083872, 83739051-83739052, 84411502, 84553520,
85181194, 85418740, 87197252, 88020545-88020546, 88021216,
88023752, 88024422, 88071013-88071014, 88755730, 89294003,
92741348-92741349, 92743744-92743745, 94017998, 95929572-95929573,
97369221, 97485310, 99685572, 100687317, 100689593,
102205779, 103403045, 104768238, 105074641, 105638643,
106115226, 106115791, 106117947, 106118512, 106120668,
106121233, 106122698, 106123954-106123955, 106125419-106125420,
106125984-106125985, 106128141, 106128706, 106186051,
106936608, 107133037, 107276378, 108007258, 109270108,
109270673, 109272829, 109273394, 109275550, 109319902,
110072175, 111250371, 111251549, 111485059, 112587333,
112588682-112588684, 114286586, 114359887, 115110935,
116807008-116807009, 116808918, 117175664, 117177512,
117178002, 117179850, 117180340-117180341, 117181588,
117182678-117182680, 117183926, 117184417, 117186264-117186265,
117186755, 117188602-117188604, 117189093, 117190341,
117193170, 117195017-117195018, 117195508, 117197355-117197357,
117197846, 117199094, 117199584, 117201432, 117201922-117201923,
117203770, 117204260-117204262, 117205508, 117206599,
117207846-117207848, 117208337, 117210185, 117210675,
117212523, 117213013-117213014, 117214261, 117215352,
117217090, 117218938, 117219428-117219429, 117221276,
117221766-117221768, 117223014, 117223505, 117225352-117225354,
117225843, 117227691, 117228181, 117229429, 117230519-117230520,
117231767, 117232258, 117234105-117234106, 117234596,
117236444, 117236934, 117238182, 117239272-117239273,
117240520, 117241011, 117242858-117242859, 117245687-117245688,
117246935, 117247426, 117249273-117249274, 117249764,
117251612, 117252102, 117253350, 117254440-117254441,
117255688, 117256179, 117258026-117258027, 117258517,
117260365, 117260855, 117262103, 117263193-117263194,
117264441, 117264932, 117266779-117266780, 117267270,

```
117269118, 117269608, 117270856, 117271946-117271947,
117275533, 117276023, 117277871, 117278361-117278363,
117279609, 117280100, 117281947-117281948, 117282438,
117284286, 117284776, 117286024, 117287114-117287116,
117288362, 117288853, 117290700-117290702, 117291191,
117293039, 117293529, 117294777, 117295867-117295869,
117297115, 117297606, 117299453-117299455, 119655644
```

□□□□□□ □120103200□ □□□ 36198288 □□□□□□ □□□□□□□ □□□□ □□□□□□□□□□□□□□ □156301488□

□□□□ □□□□□□   0

□□□ □□□□ □□□□ □□□□□□   0

□□□ □□□□ □□□□ □23□□ 36198288

□□□□□ □□□□□□   0

□□□□□ □□ □□□□□   0

□□□□ □□□□ □□□□□□□

□□□ □□□□ □□□□□□

□□□ □□□□ □□□□□□ 120103200-156301487

□□□□□ □□□□ □□□□□□

□□□□□ □□□ □□□□□□ □□□□□□

0 □□□□□□ □□□□ □□□□□□, 0 □□□□□□□□□□□ □□□□ □□□□□□

□□□□□   □□□□□□□□ □□□□□   □□□□□□ □□□□ 15881 □□□□□□□□□ □2□43   □□□□□
          □□□□□□□ □□□□□□□□□
     □□□□□□□□□□ □□□□□ □□□□□□□   □□□□□□□ □□□□□ □□□
     □□□□□□   □ □□-□□5   □□□□□ □ □□□-□□□□
     □□□□□□□□□□ □ □□□□□□□
          100□ □□□□□□ □□□□ □□ □□□ □□□□□□□ □□□□□ □□□ □□□□
          □□□□□□□□□□ □□□□□□□ □□ □□□ □□□□□□□□ □□□□□□
     □□□□□□□ □□□□□□□ □□□□ □□□ □□□□□□□□ □□□□□□□□□□ □□□□□ □□□□□□
□□□□□□□□□□□□□□□□□□□□   □□□□□ □□□□□   □□□□□□□□□□□□□□□□□□□□□□□
          □□□□□□□ □□□□□□□□□□□□□□
     □□□□□ □□□□□□ □□□□□□ 6□060□0
          □□□□□□ □22□□7□
     □□□□□□□□ □□□□□   □□□□□□   □□□□□ □□□□□□   □□□□□ □□□□
          119150   16   63   120103200   57□3 □□
          □□□□□□□ □□5 □□□□□□ □288054□ □□3□56□1 218□□□8□ □2□□□940
          □□□□□□ □□□□□□□□ 468
□□□□□□□□□□□□□□□□□□□□□□□   □□□□□□□□ □□□□□   □□□□□□□□□□□□□□□□□□□□□
          □□□□□□□ □□□□□□□□□□□□□□
     □□□□□ □□□□□□ □□380013□□
          □□□□□□ 5□□□□□□
     □□□□□□□□ □□□□□   □□□□□□   □□□□□ □□□□□□   □□□□□ □□□□
          155061   16   63   156301488   74□5 □□
          □□□□□□□ □□□-256 □□□□□□ □□□□
          □□□□□□ □□□□□□ □□□□□□□□

```
1344585     2594747     2595500     2599086     2599839     2809909
2809910     3422895     3422896     4116750     4120336     4120337
4121089     4121090     4696046     4698397     4703710     4707186
4708105     4711580     4712499     4714850     4715770     4719245
4723639     4723640     4724558     4724559     4728034     4728953
4731304     4732223     4735699     4740093     4741012     4743363
4745407     4748677     4752152     4756547     4757466     4759817
4761860     4761861     4764211     4764212     4765130     4765131
4768606     4769525     4773001     4773920     4776271     4777190
4780665     4781584     5446946     5448990     5451341     5452260
5620120     5623595     5623596     5623597     5624514     5624515
5624516     5626865     5626866     5626867     5628909     5631260
5632179     5635655     5636574     5640049     6021518     6023869
6024788     6028263     7662307     8340091     8340092     12178157
12179060    12181370    12182273    12185687    12186590    12340277
13016906    13049575    13050477    13050478    14000022    14000762
14004285    14041240    17135988    17723611    17876726    18161032
18760155    20090856    20094289    20095011    20661414    21693295
21694174    21697502    22730717    22838734    22838735    24596104
24596105    24596106    26791779    27686030    28080041    28081995
29555383    29655054    30488210    30488211    32215323    32218669
33523139    33991449    35267814    37975363    38134596    38136734
38137571    38137572    38207258    38207259    38542983    38567425
38568109    39421072    39421909    39425071    40273501    42836488
42837172    42843548    42847497    42851446    42854557    43505180
43508342    43872574    43873411    45217120    45217121    45777316
```

```
         46221189    46296219    46296220    46528674    46955925    47093653
         48537000    48537662    49911188    49911189    51017721    51769307
         51769969    51994516    51994517    53855354    55793018    55793019
         57316559    57320313    60571670    60571671    60571672    60952349
         60952350    60952993    61535962    61535963    61535964    62592910
         62593672    62596563    62597325    62600215    63140751    63140752
         63141513    63141514    63144404    63226363    63229253    63670246
         63972517    63975497
```

□□□□□□□ □□□□□□□□ 468   □□□□□□□□□ □□□□□□□□ 0
□□□□□□□ □□□□□□□□ 468
□□□□□□□ □□□□□□ □□□□□□□□□
□□□□□□□ □□□□□□□□ 468   □□□□□□□□□ □□□□□□□□ 0
3 □□□□□□□□□ □□□ □□□□□□□ □□□□□□□□ □□ 366 □□□□
287 □□□□ □□ □□□□□□ 1
56 □□□□ □□ □□□□□□ 2
23 □□□□ □□ □□□□□□ 3
468 □□□□□□□□ □□□□□□
    468 □□□□ □□□□□□ □□□ 0 □□□□□□□□ □□□-□□□□ □□□□□□
□□□□□□□□□□ □□□□□□ □□□□
□□□□□□ □□□-□□□□

□□□□□□□□		
Assertion & Expected Result		**Actual Result**
□□-01 □□□□□□ □□□□□□□□ □□□□□ □□□□□□□□□ □□□		□□ □□□□□□□□
□□-02 □□□□□□ □□ □□□□ □□□		□□ □□□□□□□□
□□-03 □□□□□□□□ □□□□□□□□□□□ □□ □□□		□□ □□□□□□□□
□□-05 □□ □□□□□ □□ □□□□□□□ □□ □□□□□ □□□□□□ □□□□ □□□		□□ □□□□□□□□
□□-06 □□□ □□□□□□□ □□□□□□□ □□□□□□□□□		□□ □□□□□□□□
□□-08 □□□ □□□□□□□ □□□□□□□□□ □□□□□□□□□		□□ □□□□□□□□
□□-09 □□□□□ □□□□□□□		□□ □□□□□□□□
□□-10 □□□□□□ □□□□ □□□□□□□ □□□□□□□□□□ □□□□□□□□		□□ □□□□□□□□
□□-01 □□□□□ □□□□ □□ □□□□□□□ □□□ □□□□□□□□□		□□ □□□□□□□□
□□-05 □□□□□□□□ □□□□□ □□□□□□□□		□□ □□□□□□□□
□□-22 □□□□ □□□□□□□□□ □□□□□□ □□ □□□□□□		□□□□□□ □□□ □□□□□□
□□-23 □□□□□□ □□□□□□□□□□ □□ □□□□□□□□		□□ □□□□□□□□
□□-24 □□□□□□ □□ □□□□□□□□ □□ □□□□□□□□□□□		□□□ □□□□□□□

□□□□□□□□□ | □□□□□□□□ □□□□□□□ □□□□□□□□
```
```

5.2.22   DA-12

Test Case DA-12 F-TALON V2.43	
□□□□ □□□□□□□□	□□-12 □□□□□□□□ □□ □□□□□□□ □□ □□□□□□ □□□□ □□□□□□ □□□□□□ □□ □□□□□□□□□□□□□□ □□□□□□
□□□□□□□□□□□□□	□□-01 □□□□ □□□□ □□□□ □□□□□□□ □□□□□□□□□□ □□□-□□ □□ □□□□□□□ □□□ □□□□□□□□ □□□□□□□□ □□-02 □□□ □□□□ □□□□□□□□ □□□□□□□□ □□□□□□□ □□□ □□-03 □□□ □□□□ □□□□□□□□ □□ □□□□□□□□□ □□□□□□□□□□□ □□□ □□-05 □□ □□□□□□ □□□□ □□□□□□□□ □□ □□□□□□□□□, □□□ □□□□ □□□□□□□ □□ □□□□□ □□□□ □□ □□□□ □□□□□□ □□□□ □□□ □□-04 □□ □□□□ □□□□ □□ □□□□□□□□ □□ □□□□□ □□□□ □□□ □□□□□ □□ □□□□□□□□□□□□ □□□□□□ □□ □□□ □□□□□ □□□□□□□□□□ □□□□□ □□ □□□□□□□ □□□ □□□□□ □□□□, □□□ □□□□ □□□□□ □□□□□□ □□□ □□□□□ □□-23 □□ □□□□ □□□□ □□□□ □□□ □□□ □□□□□□□□□ □□□□□□□□□, □□□ □□□□□□□□□□ □□ □□□□□□□□ □□□□□□□ □□ □□□ □□□ □□□□□ □□-24 □□ □□□ □□□□ □□□□□□□ □□ □ □□□□□□□□□□□ □□□□ □□□□□□□□ □□□□□□□□, □□□ □□□□□□□ □□□□□□ □□ □□□□□□□□ □□ □□□ □□□□□□□□□□ □□□□□□□□
□□□□□□ □□□□□	□□□
□□□□ □□□□□	□□□□□
□□□□ □□□□□	□□□ □□□ 1 12□45□21 2007
□□□□□□□	□□□□07-□□□□□ □□□ □□□□□□ □□□□□ □13-□□□□
□□□□□□ □□□□□	□□□ □□□□ □□□□□1□□ □ 655□9□□□□36□3□9□5□4□□8□□32□8□5□41□□9□52□ □ □□□ □□□□□ □□□5□□ □ 2□□□712□□□80□66□30□□□□0365□4579□ □ 156301488 □□□□□ □□□□□□□ □80026361856 □□□□□□ □□□□□□ □□□□ □□800□□-32□□□ □□□□□□ □ □□□-□□□□91510044□ □ □□□□□ □□□ □□□□□□ □□□□□ □□□□□ □□□ □□□□□ □□□□ □□□□□□□□□ □□□ 1 □ 000000063 156280257 0000□001□01 1023□254□63 □□□□ 07 □□□□ 2 □ 000000000 000000000 0000□000□00 0000□000□00 00 □□□□□ □□□□□ 3 □ 000000000 000000000 0000□000□00 0000□000□00 00 □□□□□ □□□□□ 4 □ 000000000 000000000 0000□000□00 0000□000□00 00 □□□□□ □□□□□ 1 156280257 □□□□□□□ 80015491584 □□□□□
□□□ □□□□□□□□□□□□	□□ □□□ □□□□ □□□□□ □□□-12□ □□□□□□ □□□□□□□□ □□□□□ □□□□□□□□□ □□□□□□ □□□ □□□□□□□ □□□□ □□ □□□□□ □□ □□□ □□□□□ □□□□□□ □□□□□□ □□□□ □□□□□ □□□□□□ □□- □□□□□□□□ □□□□□ □□□□□□□□□ □□□□□ □□□□□ □□□□□ □□□□-5
□□□□□□□□	

Assertion & Expected Result	Actual Result
□□-01 □□□□□ □□□□□□□ □□□□□ □□□□□□□□ □□□	□□ □□□□□□□□□
□□-02 □□□□□□ □□ □□□□ □□□	□□ □□□□□□□□□
□□-03 □□□□□□□□ □□□□□□□□□ □□ □□□	□□ □□□□□□□□
□□-05 □□ □□□□□ □□ □□□□□□□ □□ □□□□ □□□□□□ □□□□ □□□	□□ □□□□□□□□
□□-04 □□□□ □□□□□□□ □□ □□□□□ □□□□□□□□	□□ □□□□□□□□
□□-23 □□□□□ □□□□□□□□□□ □□ □□□□□□□□	□□ □□□□□□□□
□□-24 □□□□□ □□ □□□□□□□□ □□ □□□□□□□□□□□	□□ □□□□□□□□

| □□□□□□□□□ | □□□□□□□□ □□□□□□ □□□□□□□ |

5.2.23   DA-19

□□□□ □□□□□□□□□	□□-19 □□□□□□□□ □ □□□□□□□□□ □□□□□□ □□ □□ □□□□□□□□□ □□□□□, □□□□□□□ □□□□□□ □□□□□□□□□
□□□□□□□□□□□	□□-01 □□□ □□□□ □□□□ □□□□□□ □□□□□□□□ □□□-□□ □□ □□□□□ □□□ □□□□□□ □□□□□□□ □□-02 □□□ □□□□ □□□□□□□ □□□□□□ □□□□□ □□□ □□-03 □□□ □□□□ □□□□□□ □□ □□□□□□ □□□□□□□□ □□□ □□-04 □□ □□□□ □□□□□□ □□ □□□□□□, □□□ □□□□ □□□□□ □ □□□□ □□ □□□ □□□□□ □□□□□□ □□-06 □□□ □□□□□□ □□□□□ □□□ □□□□□□ □□□ □□□ □□□□□ □□□□□□ □□-08 □□□ □□□□□ □□□□□□ □□□□ □□□ □□□□□ □□□□□ □□□ □□□□□ □□□□□□□□□□ □□-11 □□ □□□□□□□□, □ □□□□□ □□ □□□□□□□ □□□□□ □□ □□□□□□□□ □□ □ □□□□□□ □□□□□□ □□-13 □ □□□□□ □□ □□□□□□ □□□□□ □□□□□ □□□□□□□ □□□-□□ □□ □□□□□ □□ □□□ □□□□ □□□□□□ □□-14 □□ □□ □□□□□□□ □□□□□ □□ □□□□□□, □□□□ □□□□□ □□□□□□ □□ □□□ □□□□ □□ □□□□□□□□□ □□□□□□ □□ □□□ □□□□ □□□ □□□□□ □□ □□□ □□□□□ □□□□ □□□ □□□□□ □□□□□□□□□ □□ □□□ □□□□□□ □□□□□□ □□-18 □□ □□□□□□□, □ □□□□□ □□□□ □□ □□□□□ □□ □□□□□ □□□□□□ □□ □ □□□□□ □□-22 □□ □□□□□□□, □□□ □□□□ □□□□□□□□ □□□□ □□□□□ □□□ □ □□□□□□□□ □□□□ □□□□ □□□□□ □□ □□□□□□□□ □□□ □□□□ □□□□ □□□□□□ □□□ □□□ □□□□□ □□□□□□ □□-23 □□ □□□ □□□□ □□□□ □□□ □□□ □□□□□□□□□ □□□□□□□□, □□□ □□□□□□□□ □□ □□□□□□□□ □□□□□□□ □□ □□□ □□□ □□□□□ □□-24 □□ □□□ □□□□ □□□□□□ □□ □ □□□□□□□□□ □□□ □□□□□□ □□□□□□□□, □□□ □□□□□□□ □□□□□ □□ □□□□□□□ □□ □□□ □□□□□□□□□ □□□□□□□
□□□□□□ □□□□□	□□□
□□□□ □□□□□	□□□
□□□□ □□□□□	□□□ □□□ 1 13□11□07 2007
□□□□□□□	□□□□□41□ □□□ □22-□□□□ □□□□□ □□□□□□
□□□□□□ □□□□□	□□□ □□□□ □□□256□□ □ □□□3□□21489653□880□□□□71449□9□7□8□□4□56□6□3□□58□3□3□□□13203□1□1□ □ □□□ □□□□ □□□1□□ □ 15□□□1□307271160□8372668□□8□03□45□51□9 □ □□□ □□□□ □□□5□□ □ 0□6□8□□78□□14□202671□8□□5607□ □ 78125000 □□□□□ □□□□□□ □40000000000 □□□□□□ 65534□015□63 □□□□ □□□□□ □□□□□□ 65535□016□63 □□□□□□ □□ □□□□□□□ □□□ □□□□□ □□□□□ □□□□ □□400□□-75□□□0□ □□□□□ □ □□□-□□□□□4658355□

```
□   □□□□□ □□□ □□□□□□    □□□□□ □□□□□ □□□ □□□□□  □□□□ □□□□□□□□□ □□□□
1 □ 000000063 078107967 0000□001□01 1023□254□63 □□□□ 07 □□□□
2 □ 000000000 000000000 0000□000□00 0000□000□00    □□ □□□□□ □□□□□
3 □ 000000000 000000000 0000□000□00 0000□000□00    00 □□□□□ □□□□□
4 □ 000000000 000000000 0000□000□00 0000□000□00    00 □□□□□ □□□□□
1 078107967 □□□□□□□ 39991279104 □□□□□
```

| □□□ □□□□□□□□□□□ | □□□□□□□□□□□ □□□□□
156301488 □□□□□□□ □□□□□ □□□□ 22

□□□□□□□□□□ □□ □□□□□□□ □□ □□□□□ □□□□□
□□□□□□□ □□□□□□□□ 78125000
□□□□□□□ □□□□□□ 78125000
□□□□□□□ □□□□□□□ 0
□□□□□ □□□□□□□ 0
□□□□□ □□□□□
□□□□□□ □78125000□ □□□ 78176488 □□□□□ □□□□□□ □□□□ □□□□□□□□□ □156301488□
□□□□ □□□□□ 78176488
□□□ □□□□ □□□□ □41□□ 0
□□□ □□□□ □□□□ □22□□ 0
□□□□□ □□□□□ 0
□□□□□ □□ □□□□□ 0
□□□□ □□□□ □□□□□□ 78125000-156301487
□□□ □□□□ □□□□□□
□□□ □□□□ □□□□□
□□□□□ □□□□ □□□□□□
□□□□□ □□□ □□□□□ □□□□□□
0 □□□□□ □□□□ □□□□□□, 0 □□□□□□□□□ □□□□ □□□□□□ |

Test Case DA-19 F-TALON V2.43

□□□□□ □□□□□□□□□ □□□□□ □□□□□□ □□□□ 15881 □□□□□□□□□ □2□43 □□□□□
□□□□□□□ □□□□□□□□□
□□□□□□□□□□ □□□□□ □□□□□□□ □□□□□□□ □□□□□ □□□
□□□□□□ □ □□-□□5 □□□□□ □ □□□□-4
□□□□□□□□□□ □ □□□□□□□
100□ □□□□□□ □□□□ □□ □□□ □□□□□□□ □□□□□ □□□ □□□□
□□□□□□□□□□ □□□□□□□ □□ □□□ □□□□□□□□ □□□□□□
□□□□□□□ □□□□□□□□ □□□□ □□□□ □□□□ □□□□□ □□□ □□□□□ □□□□□□□□□
□□□□□□□□□□□□□□□□□□□ □□□□□ □□□□□ □□□□□□□□□□□□□□□□□□□□
□□□□□□□□ □□□□□□□□□□□□□
□□□□□ □□□□□□ □□□ □□400□□-75□□□0
□□□□□□□ □□-□□□□□4658355
□□□□□□□□ □□□□□ □□□□□□□ □□□□□ □□□□□□□ □□□□□ □□□□
77504 16 63 78125000 37□3 □□
□□□□□□□□ □□5 □□□□□□ 0□6□8□□7 8□□□14□2 02671□□8 □□□5607□
□□□□□□□ □□□□□□□□ 0
□□□□□□□□□□□□□□□□□□□□□□□ □□□□□□□□□□ □□□□□ □□□□□□□□□□□□□□□□□□
□□□□□□□ □□□□□□□□□□□□□
□□□□□ □□□□□□ □□380013□□
□□□□□□□ 5□□□□731
□□□□□□□□ □□□□□ □□□□□□□ □□□□□ □□□□□□□ □□□□□ □□□□
155061 16 63 156301488 74□5 □□
□□□□□□□□ □□□-256 □□□□□□ □□□□
□□□□□□□ □□□□□□□□ 0
□□□□□□□□ □□□□□ □□□□
□□□□□ □□□□-5

	Assertion & Expected Result	Actual Result
□□□□□□□□	□□-01 □□□□□□ □□□□□□□□ □□□□□ □□□□□□□□ □□□	□□ □□□□□□□□
	□□-02 □□□□□□ □□ □□□□ □□□	□□ □□□□□□□□
	□□-03 □□□□□□□□ □□□□□□□□□□ □□ □□□	□□ □□□□□□□□
	□□-04 □ □□□□□ □□ □□□□□□□□	□□ □□□□□□□□
	□□-06 □□□ □□□□□□□ □□□□□□ □□□□□□□□	□□ □□□□□□□□
	□□-08 □□□ □□□□□□□ □□□□□□□□ □□□□□□□□	□□ □□□□□□□□
	□□-11 □ □□□□□ □□ □□□□□□ □□□□□ □□□□□□□□□□□	□□ □□□□□□□□
	□□-13 □□□□□ □□□□□□ □□□□□ □□□□□□□□ □□□	□□ □□□□□□□□
	□□-14 □□ □□□□□□□□ □□□□□ □□ □□□□□□□□	□□ □□□□□□□□
	□□-18 □□□□□□ □□□□□□□ □□□ □□□□□□□	□□ □□□□□□□□
	□□-22 □□□□ □□□□□□□□□ □□□□□□ □□ □□□□□□	□□□□□□ □□□ □□□□□□
	□□-23 □□□□□□ □□□□□□□□□□ □□ □□□□□□□□	□□ □□□□□□□□
	□□-24 □□□□□□ □□ □□□□□□□□□ □□ □□□□□□□□□□□	□□ □□□□□□□□

| □□□□□□□□□□ | □□□□□□□□□ □□□□□□ □□□□□□□□ |

About the National Institute of Justice

NIJ is the research, development, and evaluation agency of the U.S. Department of Justice. NIJ's mission is to advance scientific research, development, and evaluation to enhance the administration of justice and public safety. NIJ's principal authorities are derived from the Omnibus Crime Control and Safe Streets Act of 1968, as amended (see 42 U.S.C. §§ 3721–3723).

The NIJ Director is appointed by the President and confirmed by the Senate. The Director establishes the Institute's objectives, guided by the priorities of the Office of Justice Programs, the U.S. Department of Justice, and the needs of the field. The Institute actively solicits the views of criminal justice and other professionals and researchers to inform its search for the knowledge and tools to guide policy and practice.

Strategic Goals

NIJ has seven strategic goals grouped into three categories:

Creating relevant knowledge and tools

1. Partner with State and local practitioners and policymakers to identify social science research and technology needs.
2. Create scientific, relevant, and reliable knowledge—with a particular emphasis on terrorism, violent crime, drugs and crime, cost-effectiveness, and community-based efforts—to enhance the administration of justice and public safety.
3. Develop affordable and effective tools and technologies to enhance the administration of justice and public safety.

Dissemination

4. Disseminate relevant knowledge and information to practitioners and policymakers in an understandable, timely, and concise manner.
5. Act as an honest broker to identify the information, tools, and technologies that respond to the needs of stakeholders.

Agency management

6. Practice fairness and openness in the research and development process.
7. Ensure professionalism, excellence, accountability, cost-effectiveness, and integrity in the management and conduct of NIJ activities and programs.

Program Areas

In addressing these strategic challenges, the Institute is involved in the following program areas: crime control and prevention, including policing; drugs and crime; justice systems and offender behavior, including corrections; violence and victimization; communications and information technologies; critical incident response; investigative and forensic sciences, including DNA; less-than-lethal technologies; officer protection; education and training technologies; testing and standards; technology assistance to law enforcement and corrections agencies; field testing of promising programs; and international crime control.

In addition to sponsoring research and development and technology assistance, NIJ evaluates programs, policies, and technologies. NIJ communicates its research and evaluation findings through conferences and print and electronic media.

To find out more about the National Institute of Justice, please visit:

http://www.ojp.usdoj.gov/nij

or contact:

National Criminal Justice
 Reference Service
P.O. Box 6000
Rockville, MD 20849–6000
800–851–3420
http://www.ncjrs.gov

www.ingramcontent.com/pod-product-compliance
Lightning Source LLC
Chambersburg PA
CBHW080530290526
45790CB00006B/2358